GEORGE
WASHINGTON

TIME

© 2018 Time Inc. Books

Published by Liberty Street,
an imprint of Time Inc. Books, a division of Meredith Corporation
225 Liberty Street
New York, NY 10281

LIBERTY STREET and Time Books
are trademarks of Time Inc.

ISBN: 978-1-68330-849-2

First edition, 2018
1 QGV 18
10 9 8 7 6 5 4 3 2 1

We welcome your comments and suggestions about Time Inc. Books.
Please write to us at:

Time Inc. Books
Attention: Book Editors
P.O. Box 62310
Tampa, FL 33662-2310
(800) 765-6400

timeincbooks.com

Time Inc. Books products may be purchased for business or promotional
use. For information on bulk purchases, please contact Christi Crowley in
the Special Sales Department at (845) 895-9858.

HEROES OF HISTORY

GEORGE
WASHINGTON

Contents

In which our hero adventures to the American West and finds the love of his life.

First, let's dispense with the folklore: you know that story about George Washington and the cherry tree? When he was just a boy, George chopped down a cherry tree in this yard. When his father confronted him, little George confessed, "I cannot tell a lie." Or so the story goes. All historians agree: it never happened. There's also a story about Washington throwing a silver dollar across the Potomac River near his home at Mount Vernon. But that's not true either.

1732
BORN ON
FEBRUARY 22

1748
FIRST
SURVEY
EXPEDITION

There are plenty of legends about Washington that don't hold up. But the funny thing is that his real life story—the one that is 100% true—doesn't need any help. Washington led the Continental Army to victory in the Revolutionary War. He helped write the Constitution. And he became the first president of the United States.

Real-life George Washington had one of the most adventurous, eventful, and important lives in history.

A 19TH−CENTURY ENGRAVING IMAGINES THE YOUNG WASHINGTON WITH HIS FATHER, AUGUSTINE.

George Washington was born on February 22, 1732, on a farm at Popes Creek in Westmoreland County, Virginia. Though Washington was of English ancestry, the links that bound his family to England were weak by the time of his birth. His great-grandfather John Washington had arrived in 1656. George's father, Augustine, was John Washington's

1754−1758
SERVED IN THE FRENCH AND INDIAN WAR

1759
MARRIED MARTHA DANDRIDGE CUSTIS

grandson. Augustine moved back to England when he was four. But he returned to Virginia to grow tobacco as an adult.

In 1731, Augustine married Mary Johnson Ball. Mary had been orphaned at an early age and was raised by a family friend, George Eskridge. Because he had treated her with great kindness, Mary gave his name to her son.

Little George grew up in wealth and comfort. When he was 3, the Washingtons moved 60 miles up the Potomac, to Little Hunting Creek. There they lived in a newly built farmhouse on a hilltop overlooking the river. They moved again three years later, to a larger house called Ferry Farm. By that time, Augustine owned nearly 10,000 acres of land and 50 slaves.

WASHINGTON'S HALF BROTHER LAWRENCE.

Despite his family's prosperity, George would never go to college. When George was 11 years old, his father died. George inherited Ferry Farm and some other properties (as well as ten slaves), but he could not claim his inheritance until he was an adult. That meant there was no money to send him away to school.

After Augustine's death, George's half brother Lawrence, who was 14 years older, became a father figure to him. Lawrence inherited the plantation at Little Hunting Creek, which he would rename Mount Vernon. When Lawrence married the daughter of William Fairfax, a wealthy aristocrat who lived near Mount Vernon, George began to spend time with the Fairfaxes as well. They would help him in his career as he grew older.

When George was 14, the Fairfaxes found him a position in the British navy. But George's mother learned that British sailors in the navy looked down on their colonial peers. George's plans were scuttled.

Two years later, George got to go on the adventure he had been looking for. William Fairfax's cousin was Lord Thomas Fairfax, an English nobleman. Lord Fairfax owned 5 million acres of land. George joined a team that set out to survey Fairfax's land in western Virginia. At the time, western Virginia was the western frontier of America. Camping and bushwhacking through the wilderness, George found a job that suited him.

He started a diary, called *Journal of My Journey over the Mountains*, in which he wrote his impressions of the hardships and glories of the natural world that he found in the Shenandoah Valley. Over the next three years, he returned

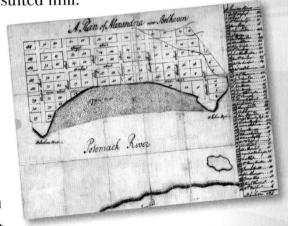

A SURVEY OF THE TOWN OF ALEXANDRIA, VIRGINIA, DRAWN BY YOUNG WASHINGTON IN 1749.

repeatedly for surveying trips for the Fairfaxes and others. George learned an important lesson: he realized that America's destiny lay in the western wilderness. And with the money he made from surveying, he was able to buy 1,459 acres of land by the time he was 18 years old.

By this time, Washington stood somewhere between 6 feet and 6-feet-2, weighing 175 pounds, with a pale complexion and blue eyes. He had the powerful legs of an experienced rider and sizable hands and feet.

Washington was an awkward youth. We know from his flirtatious letters and gushing romantic poetry that as a young man he developed fixations on any number of girls. One would haunt him for years. Washington got to know Sarah "Sally" Fairfax, two years his senior and a daughter of one of Virginia's wealthiest

A 19TH-CENTURY ARTIST DEPICTS WASHINGTON, IN THE COMPANY OF AMERICAN INDIANS, AS A SURVEYOR IN THE OHIO VALLEY WILDERNESS.

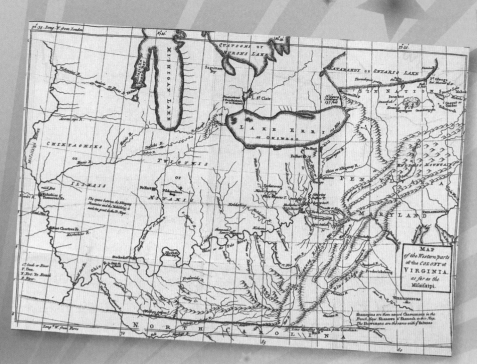

THE WESTERN TERRITORIES THAT WASHINGTON TRAVELED AS A YOUNG MAN, AND THAT HE RECOGNIZED AS KEY TO AMERICA'S FUTURE.

families, at a very inconvenient time—she had just married his friend and neighbor George William Fairfax in December 1748. Sometime early in the following year, Washington was in love. Some of their later correspondence is a good deal warmer than "neighborly," and he carried her seriously in his affections for the rest of his life, as a letter written many years later attests.

It was also in 1749 that Washington's half brother Lawrence developed a severe cough, a first sign of tuberculosis. When he decided two years later to attempt a cure in the warmer climate of Barbados, he invited George to join him. On that trip, the only one he would ever make abroad, George took sick as well, with a severe case of smallpox. He recovered fully, and though it left him with a faint sprinkling of scars on his nose, the episode was a blessing in disguise. For the rest of his life, he would be immune to one of the deadliest diseases of the 18th century.

Unfortunately, the visit to Barbados was of little use to Lawrence. In July 1752, he died at Mount Vernon. Though Lawrence's widow, Ann, continued to live there for a time with their daughter, the 2,500-acre plantation now became part of the estate that would eventually pass to George.

Lawrence's death marked the start of George Washington's long military career. He took over Lawrence's former post as an adjutant general of Virginia, a high office in the colony's militia. Although he had no real military experience, Washington now held the rank of major.

LAWRENCE'S DEATH MARKED THE START OF GEORGE WASHINGTON'S LONG MILITARY CAREER.

In October 1753, Virginia's royal lieutenant governor, Robert Dinwiddie, asked the 21-year-old Washington to lead a small band of militiamen into the Ohio Valley. This huge area included present-day Ohio, Indiana, western Pennsylvania, and West Virginia. Even as British settlers were moving west into the territory, French hunters, trappers, and soldiers were flowing south from Canada in large numbers. To support them, and to solidify its claim to the region, France had decided to establish a chain of forts between Lake Erie and the Ohio River. But the entire region was also claimed by Britain's King George II, and Britain had decided to begin its own campaign of fort construction.

As a royal emissary, Washington had the job of carrying a letter to the French, warning them to leave.

By this time, the Ohio Valley was one of several places around the world where France and England were competing. It was a simmering fight that would soon explode into the Seven Years' War. The part of the struggle that took place in North America became known as the French and Indian War. Washington, still an obscure young colonial officer, would unintentionally start it.

In November, Washington entered the Ohio Valley, the beginning of a long trek in what quickly became winter conditions. He and his party of six men were joined along the way by four Iroquois, including a tribal chief the British called the Half King. By December, they had arrived at Fort Le Boeuf, a flimsy French outpost near what is now Waterford, Pennsylvania. There, the French received Washington with great ceremony, but also with the inconvenient news that they would not leave. While he was there, Washington noticed that the French had hundreds of canoes ready to attack the British once weather permitted.

Over the next several weeks, Washington and one of his party, an experienced guide and surveyor named Christopher Gist, struggled together over icy rivers back to Williamsburg, Virginia's colonial capital, to warn Dinwiddie that the French were preparing to invade. On their arrival, Dinwiddie urged Washington to edit his diaries of the expedition into a report. He hoped it might encourage support among the colonists for the idea of building a British fort at the Forks of the Ohio—the place where

ON THE RETURN FROM WARNING THE FRENCH THAT THE OHIO VALLEY WAS CLAIMED BY ENGLAND, WASHINGTON AND A COMPANION, CHRISTOPHER GIST, CROSSED THE ICY ALLEGHENY RIVER.

the Allegheny and Monongahela Rivers meet to form the Ohio. When Washington's report appeared in colonial newspapers—and then as a pamphlet in Britain called *The Journal of Major George Washington*—it provided readers with their first detailed picture of the wild country just beyond Virginia's settled coastline. And though Washington kept himself largely out of the story, it made the name George Washington known on both sides of the Atlantic.

Dinwiddie succeeded in getting Virginia's colonial legislature, called the House of Burgesses, to agree to send a force of 300 men west to confront the French. Dinwiddie wanted to make Washington commander, but Washington, knowing too well that he lacked military experience, refused the offer. Colonel Joshua Fry would lead them; Washington was named second-in-command and given the rank of lieutenant colonel.

In April 1754, Washington headed out with 159 inexperienced militiamen to reinforce an advance guard that was building a small fort at the Forks. Fry planned to join him with 100 more men. But on the way to the fort, Washington learned that 1,000 French soldiers had seized it, sent the puny British contingent packing, and renamed the place Fort Duquesne.

Arriving near the Forks in May, Washington was reunited with the Iroquois chief called the Half King and a band of his warriors. When they happened upon a party of 35 French soldiers, Washington decided to attack.

It was the first firefight of the French and Indian War. It was also the moment that George Washington realized that he liked the heat of battle. He later wrote home to his brother John,

"I heard the bullets whistle, and, believe me, there is something charming in the sound."

In the fight that followed, Washington's men quickly overwhelmed the French, killing or wounding ten—including their commander, Joseph Coulon de Villiers, Sieur de Jumonville. Before Jumonville died, he had time to protest that he was traveling to present to the British a letter explaining his king's claim to the Ohio Valley—the very thing Washington had done to the French the previous year. Jumonville was a diplomat, and his killing was a grievous breach of international relations.

The battle made Washington something of a hero in the colonies. But the British viewed him differently. They saw him as a raw young colonial who had acted rashly. To the French, he was the cold-blooded killer of a royal envoy. Meanwhile, Colonel Fry, the expedition leader whom Washington was expected to join, died in a riding mishap. Washington, still camped in the Ohio Valley and now a colonel, found himself in full command, in the job he had insisted he was unprepared for. He was right.

Convinced that his small band could withstand the much larger French force he knew was headed his way, Washington had his men build a circular stockade in an open field. He called it Fort Necessity. When the French arrived—under the command of Jumonville's furious brother—they found it easy to position themselves around the stockade and pour musket fire into it. To make matters worse, at the end of a long, bloody day, July 3, Washington signed terms of surrender that referred (in French) to the "assassination" of Jumonville. With that, he effectively

FOR THIS 1772 PORTRAIT BY CHARLES WILLSON PEALE, WASHINGTON WORE THE UNIFORM OF HIS SERVICE IN THE FRENCH AND INDIAN WAR MORE THAN A DECADE EARLIER.

AN ENGRAVING SHOWS COLONEL WASHINGTON CONSULTING WITH FELLOW OFFICERS ON JULY 3, 1754, ABOUT WHETHER TO SURRENDER TO FRENCH FORCES THAT HAD OVERWHELMED FORT NECESSITY.

acknowledged the Frenchman's diplomatic mission and thus placed blame on Britain for starting the war. It was an important blunder. For the rest of his life, he would insist he had been misled by a translator's error.

But Washington was already a hero to his countrymen. As the French and even the British continued to denounce him, Virginia's House of Burgesses issued a proclamation praising him and his fellow officers at Fort Necessity.

War between England and France was now all but officially declared. But Washington soon learned his Virginia regiment would not become part of the British Army. Instead, his band would be broken up, with colonial officers allowed to hold no rank higher than captain. Rather than accept a diminished rank, Washington resigned his commission and returned to Mount Vernon.

He would not stay there for long. As he wrote to a friend, "My inclinations are strongly bent to arms." In February 1755, British Major General Edward Braddock arrived in Virginia with nearly 3,000 men, sent by London to confront the French in the Ohio Valley and eventually seize all of French Canada. Hoping that Braddock might become the next in his line of influential patrons, Washington agreed—over his mother's fierce opposition—to serve Braddock as an aide-de-camp, a personal assistant in the field.

On July 9, an advance force of 1,400 British soldiers, including Washington, began to cross the Monongahela River not far from Fort Duquesne. What they did not know—until the air filled with war whoops—was that 900 French soldiers and their American Indian allies awaited them. Braddock, following the European style of battle, kept his troops in tight field formation. In the battle that followed, the British, arranged like sitting ducks in their compact platoons, were wiped out. Scores of Virginia militiamen were cut down accidentally by friendly fire from the disoriented British. Braddock, badly wounded, died three days later. Washington performed with extraordinary bravery that day, continuing to fight even after having two horses shot out from under him, but it was no use. Among the British and their American allies, there were 900 dead and wounded. Only 39 French soldiers were wounded.

The disaster on the Monongahela left Washington all the more convinced

> WASHINGTON PERFORMED WITH EXTRAORDINARY BRAVERY THAT DAY, CONTINUING TO FIGHT EVEN AFTER HAVING TWO HORSES SHOT OUT FROM UNDER HIM.

ON JULY 9, 1755, AT THE BATTLE OF THE MONONGAHELA, BRITISH MAJOR GENERAL EDWARD BRADDOCK IS MORTALLY WOUNDED. WASHINGTON (ON HORSEBACK) LOOKS ON.

that the agile, forest-fighting tactics of the American Indians were the ones best suited to the colonies. (He would write later of the American Indians, "I cannot conceive the best white men to be equal to them in the woods.") It was an insight that would serve him well in later years.

In August, Washington was named commander of the newly reestablished Virginia Regiment. Under his training, his men became a disciplined fighting force. Discipline would be strict in his regiment, enforced with a whip—flogging was the penalty even for swearing. For deserters there was the noose. To instill regimental pride, Washington mandated that all officers wear uniforms of blue coats with scarlet waistcoats. Always sensitive to signs of disrespect toward colonial soldiers—himself in particular—he was furious that he and his troops were paid less than British men and officers. In a letter to Dinwiddie that sounded an early note of the complaints that would lead to the American Revolution, he wrote, "We cannot conceive that because we are Americans, we should therefore be deprived of the benefits common to British subjects."

The chief duty of Washington's regiment was to protect the 350-mile-long Virginia frontier from American Indian attacks. From the first, he complained that the colonial legislature had failed to give him enough men or supplies for the job. But most of the fighting in the French and Indian War was happening farther north, in Canada.

Washington would take part in only one significant campaign of the war. In the spring of 1758, Britain shipped across the Atlantic a force of 7,000 men, more than twice the size of the one Braddock had commanded. The mission was to retake Fort Duquesne from the French.

The outcome was satisfactory but not exactly glorious. Shortly before the overwhelming British force arrived at Fort Duquesne, the outnumbered French simply set fire to the place and headed off down the Ohio River. The British constructed a new stockade there and called it Fort Pitt, after British prime minister William Pitt. The city of Pittsburgh would eventually grow up around it.

ON JANUARY 6, 1759, WASHINGTON MARRIED THE RECENTLY WIDOWED—AND VERY WEALTHY— MARTHA DANDRIDGE CUSTIS AT HER HOME.

With that, Washington decided it was time to resign his commission and return to civilian life. In July, he had been elected to the House of Burgesses, and he also had an important personal matter to attend to at home. In March, he had begun courting the wealthiest widow in Virginia, Martha Dandridge Custis. Introduced by a friend, she and Washington had a lightning courtship. Washington ordered a ring just months after meeting Martha. On January 6, 1759, they married at her home.

It was called the White House.

Home Sweet Home

AFTER THEIR MARRIAGE, GEORGE AND MARTHA WASHINGTON MOVED TO MOUNT VERNON. WASHINGTON HAD INHERITED THE ESTATE THROUGH THE WILL OF HIS BELOVED OLDER HALF BROTHER LAWRENCE.

IN 1858, THE ARTIST JOACHIM FERDINAND RICHARDT PAINTED THIS VIEW OF THE MANSION HOUSE.

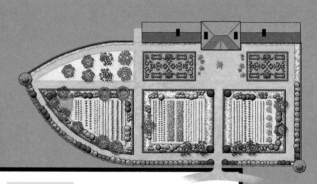

THE GARDEN LAYOUT AT MOUNT VERNON.

WASHINGTON ACTED AS HIS OWN ARCHITECT AT MOUNT VERNON, AND HE POURED WHATEVER MONEY HE HAD INTO THE HOUSE. HE DOUBLED THE SIZE OF THE HOUSE AND RELOCATED THE MAIN ENTRANCE SO THAT IT FACED AWAY FROM THE POTOMAC RIVER AND TOWARD THE WILDERNESS LANDS THAT SO FASCINATED HIM. BRICK-WALLED RECTANGULAR GARDENS WERE LAID OUT IN FRONT.

WHEN WASHINGTON INHERITED THE ESTATE, IT WAS 3,500 ACRES (ABOUT 5.5 SQUARE MILES) PLUS ADJOINING PROPERTIES. BY THE TIME HE DEPARTED FOR THE REVOLUTIONARY WAR 15 YEARS LATER, HE HAD INCREASED IT TO 6,000 ACRES.

OVER TIME, IT WOULD INCLUDE VINEYARDS AND ORCHARDS, A DAIRY, A SAWMILL, A FLOURMILL, AND A DISTILLERY. WITH THE POTOMAC TEEMING WITH BASS, CARP, HERRING, AND SHAD, WASHINGTON DEPLOYED A SMALL FLEET OF BOATS THAT HAULED IN TONS OF FISH.

A DETAILED MAP OF THE FIVE FARMS AT MOUNT VERNON.

MOUNT VERNON WAS NOT A SINGLE LARGE PLANTATION BUT A COLLECTION OF FIVE FARMS, INCLUDING THE ONE CONNECTED TO THE MAIN HOUSE. TO SUPERVISE THE SLAVE LABOR THAT MADE THE FARMS RUN, EACH FARM HAD ITS OWN OVERSEER, SOME OF WHOM WERE ENSLAVED THEMSELVES. WHEN HE WAS AT HOME, WASHINGTON SPENT MUCH OF HIS TIME RIDING A CIRCUIT AMONG HIS FARMS OF 20 MILES OR MORE TO INSPECT CROPS, WOODLANDS, FENCES, AND DITCHES.

THE WASHINGTONS ENTERTAIN ON THE PORCH AT MOUNT VERNON.

AT MOUNT VERNON, WASHINGTON LED A WELL-REGULATED EXISTENCE. HE ROSE AT DAWN AND BREAKFASTED ON TEA, HONEY, AND CORN CAKES, THEN LEFT ON HIS INSPECTION ROUNDS. FAMOUS FOR HIS PUNCTUALITY, HE COULD BE COUNTED ON TO RETURN BY 2:45 P.M. TO BE IN TIME FOR SUPPER AT 3:00, WHEN THERE WERE ALMOST ALWAYS GUESTS AT THE TABLE. THE LARGEST MEAL OF THE DAY, SUPPER WAS OFTEN BUILT AROUND FISH CAUGHT STRAIGHT FROM THE POTOMAC AND THREE OR FOUR GLASSES OF WINE.

AFTER SUPPER, WASHINGTON MIGHT RETIRE TO HIS LIBRARY TO WRITE LETTERS AND HANDLE THE ESTATE'S WELL-KEPT RECORDS. THERE WOULD BE A LIGHT DINNER LATER. BY 9:00 P.M., HE WAS IN BED. ON DAYS THAT WERE NOT TAKEN UP BY THE ROUTINES OF WORK, HE LOVED TO HUNT. A SKILLED HORSEMAN, HE ALSO BRED HIS OWN HOUNDS.

WASHINGTON'S BEDROOM.

A HARPSICHORD FROM THE ESTATE.

THE STABLE WITH AN 18TH-CENTURY CARRIAGE.

26

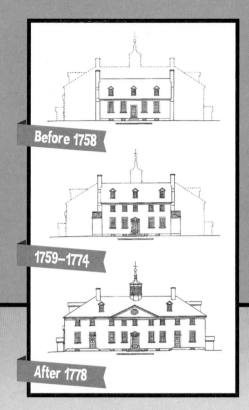

Before 1758

1759–1774

After 1778

IN 1775, JUST BEFORE HE LEFT TO HEAD THE CONTINENTAL ARMY, WASHINGTON BEGAN ANOTHER MAJOR RENOVATION OF MOUNT VERNON—ONE THAT, WHEN IT WAS COMPLETED, PRODUCED THE SPLENDID MANSION WE KNOW TODAY.

THE ARTWORK AT TOP LEFT DEPICTS MOUNT VERNON WHEN WASHINGTON FIRST MOVED THERE. BELOW IT, THE RENOVATIONS HE MADE AFTER HIS RETURN FROM THE FRENCH AND INDIAN WAR. THE BOTTOM DRAWING AND PHOTO BELOW SHOW THE HOUSE AS IT APPEARS TODAY.

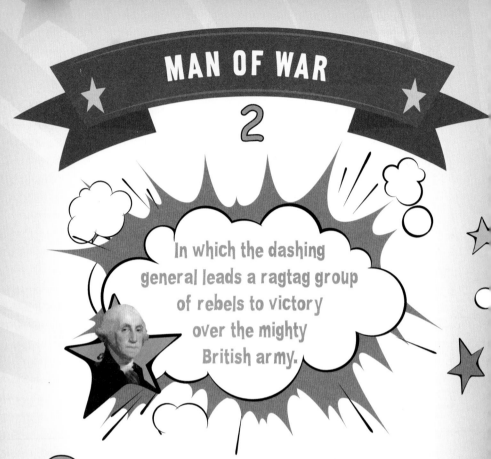

MAN OF WAR

2

In which the dashing general leads a ragtag group of rebels to victory over the mighty British army.

Over the next 16 years, Washington enjoyed the life of a Virginia planter and country squire. With the money and land—about 8,000 acres—that Martha brought to their marriage, he was now one of the wealthiest men in Virginia.

Washington also worked to get more land in the western wilderness that he had grown to love. Even when King George III declared in 1763 that virtually all land west of the Appalachian Mountains to the Mississippi River was an Indian reservation closed

1775
CHOSEN AS COMMANDER OF THE CONTINENTAL ARMY

1776
CROSSED THE DELAWARE RIVER

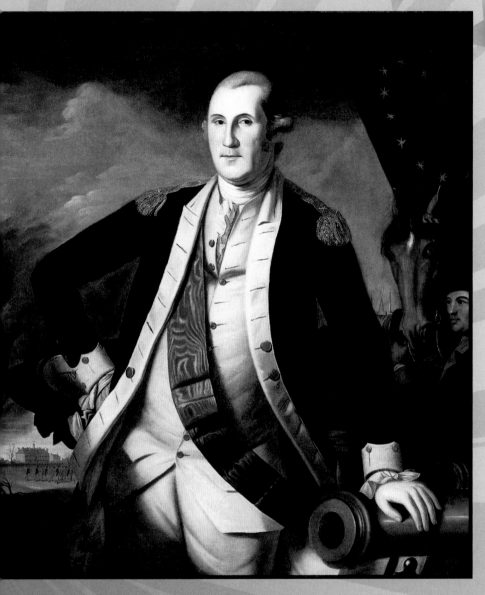

CHARLES WILLSON PEALE PAINTED WASHINGTON SEVEN TIMES. THIS PORTRAIT FROM 1779 REPRESENTS HIM AFTER HIS VICTORY AT THE BATTLE OF PRINCETON TWO YEARS EARLIER.

1777–1778
SURVIVED A
BITTER WINTER AT
VALLEY FORGE

1781
BRITISH
SURRENDERED AT
YORKTOWN

to white settlement, Washington didn't stop. He launched a real estate partnership that petitioned the British Parliament to grant it 2.5 million acres on both sides of the Ohio River. The petition did not succeed, but Washington had another plan. When Lieutenant Governor Dinwiddie had been looking for men to enlist in the Virginia Regiment during the French and Indian War, he had promised to give western land to men who joined early. Washington forced Parliament to make good on that promise, and added to his property.

George and Martha would have no children of their own. Martha had two children from her first marriage: a son, Jacky, who was 4 when she remarried, and a daughter, Patsy, who was 2. Jacky grew up spoiled and pampered, with no interest in learning and little discipline from Washington, who left him to his mother's charge. Patsy suffered from epilepsy and died at the age of 17, a devastating blow to her mother and stepfather.

The Washingtons spent a lot of time entertaining. In some years, they played host to hundreds of visitors. Washington's wealth permitted him to order fine wines and luxury goods from London. A London tailor sent him his elegant clothing. But there was one popular fashion of the time that he did not follow: he preferred not to wear a wig. Most of the time, his reddish-brown hair was neatly powdered, then tied back simply with a single ribbon.

When he was 26, Washington was elected as a representative to the House of Burgesses. With two representatives from each settlement in Virginia, the House of Burgesses made laws and distributed supplies. But any of its rules could be changed or shot down by the

British House of Lords, the king of England, or the governor of Virginia. As a representative, Washington would experience the growing frustration the American colonists felt toward the British government. Much of the strain grew out of Britain's financial problems after the French and Indian War, which ended formally in 1763. The costly war had left Britain in serious debt. It was so high that half the government's annual budget was devoted to interest payments. The British Parliament felt that the American colonists had benefited from the war, since it had made them safer from the French. So they turned to the colonies to help them pay the debt.

In 1765, Parliament passed the Stamp Act, which imposed a tax on legal documents, newspapers, and even playing cards. To many Americans, Washington among them, this was a plain violation of the long tradition that only the colonies' own legislature could impose taxes on them. The Stamp Act set off a storm of protest, and Parliament repealed it just one year later.

AS A REPRESENTATIVE, WASHINGTON WOULD EXPERIENCE THE GROWING FRUSTRATION THE AMERICAN COLONISTS FELT TOWARD THE BRITISH GOVERNMENT.

A PAMPHLET PUBLISHED IN 1764 BY RHODE ISLAND PATRIOT STEPHEN HOPKINS LAYS OUT THE CASE AGAINST THE STAMP ACT.

THE

R I G H T S

OF

C O L O N I E S

EXAMINED.

PUBLISHED BY AUTHORITY.

PROVIDENCE:
PRINTED BY *WILLIAM GODDARD*,
M.DCC.LXV.

IN NOVEMBER 1765, RIOTS OCCURRED IN NEW YORK CITY IN RESPONSE TO BRITAIN'S ADOPTION OF THE STAMP ACT.

But in 1767, Parliament returned with the Townshend Acts. These taxed a range of British imports, including paint, paper, glass, and tea. In response to the Townshend Acts, Washington presented a proposal at the House of Burgesses calling for a boycott of British manufactured goods, as well as a stop to the slave trade. As a young man, he had described England—a place where he had never set foot—as "home," but as he moved into his thirties, Washington felt a growing sense of separation from Britain. And though he didn't yet feel that the colonies must be independent from Britain, he began to entertain the idea that war was a possibility.

Eventually Parliament rolled back the Townshend Acts, too, all except for one very important part: the tax on tea was left in place.

The tea tax was despised all over the colonies, and on December 16, 1773, colonists in Massachusetts decided to show the king exactly what they thought of it. Disguised as American Indians, a group of about 60 men climbed aboard a ship in Boston Harbor and dumped 342 chests of tea, which belonged to the British East India Company, into the bay.

The fight between the colonies and Britain escalated quickly after that. Britain passed a series of laws to punish the colonies. They became known as the Intolerable Acts. One shut down the port of Boston. Another changed Massachusetts's charter, making the colony subject to military rule and requiring that any town meetings be approved by the British government.

In September 1774, the colonies convened the First Continental Congress in Philadelphia, Pennsylvania, to plot their response. Washington was one of seven delegates sent by Virginia. Although he was largely silent during the debates, he gave his strong support when the Congress approved a boycott of British goods.

On April 19, 1775, the tension between the colonies and Britain led to gunfire. A company of 700 British soldiers marched to Concord, Massachusetts, to destroy a stockpile of weapons there. The soldiers had hoped to surprise the colonists, but the American patriots had been warned by spies from Boston. In the town of Lexington, about 6 miles from Concord, a group of 77 minutemen (so called

ON APRIL 19, 1775, THE TENSION BETWEEN THE COLONIES AND BRITAIN LED TO GUNFIRE.

ON JUNE 15, 1775, WASHINGTON APPEARED BEFORE THE SECOND CONTINENTAL CONGRESS TO ACCEPT HIS APPOINTMENT AS COMMANDER IN CHIEF.

because they had pledged to take up arms at a minute's notice) blocked the soldiers' path. The Battles of Lexington and Concord were the first of the American Revolution.

A month later, on May 4, 1775, Washington left Mount Vernon in his elegant handmade carriage. He was traveling to Philadelphia to attend the Second Continental Congress. He would not see his beloved home again for eight years.

To remind other delegates that he was a seasoned military man, Washington arrived at the Congress in his blue-and-buff uniform from the French and Indian War. But they needed no reminding. On

June 15, the Congress unanimously selected him to be commander in chief of a "continental army" drawn from all the colonies.

When his appointment was announced the next day, Washington humbly told the delegates, "My abilities and military experience may not be equal to the extensive and important trust"—but he promised that he would "exert every power . . . for the support of the glorious cause." He also refused the monthly salary of $500 the Congress offered.

Compared with the British officers whom Washington would be up against, he had very little experience. He had never led an army. In fact, he'd never led more than a regiment. He had also been placed at the head of an army that barely existed. Arriving in Cambridge, Massachusetts, in July, Washington set about trying to impose order on an ill-trained force of about 14,500 New Englanders. Men in the Continental Army elected their own officers, then frequently ignored them. Washington described them to his brother Samuel as "a numerous army of provincials under very little command, discipline, or order." Guns at the time were muzzle loaded. A soldier had to drop a ball into the muzzle of his rifle, along with some gunpowder. It was the explosive power of the gunpowder that made guns—and cannons—fire. The entire army had just 36 barrels of gunpowder, a fact Washington worked hard to hide from the British.

And as bad as his men were, it was worse still that he could not count on holding on to them for long. Resistant to the idea of a standing army, which they feared could become a tool for tyranny, Congress had decided that soldiers should enlist for just 12-month tours of duty. At the beginning of every year, Washington would have to assemble a new army.

This ragtag band of would-be warriors did catch one break. A few weeks before Washington's arrival, British and American forces had fought the Battle of Bunker Hill in Massachusetts. The British had overwhelmed American fighters and taken the hill. But British casualties in that "victory" were so high—more than 1,000 killed or wounded—that their officers decided to avoid future attacks on entrenched American positions.

The British instead opted to hunker down in Boston. But Washington yearned for a proper battle. He was required to get approval from a council of war, made up of his military officers, before he made major moves. On September 11, 1775, he called a meeting and presented a plan for an assault on Boston by flat-bottomed boats. Rightly sensing disaster, his generals rejected the idea. They would shoot down several more ideas during the coming months.

But Washington had already launched another bold plan. He sent 1,200 of his men north under the command of a daredevil Connecticut colonel named Benedict Arnold. The regiment would attempt to capture Quebec, which had fallen under British control at the close of the French and Indian War. But Washington's scheme was badly timed. To reach Quebec, the regiment would have to slog through hundreds of miles of wilderness. Setting out at the start of winter to cross what was soon snow-packed Maine wilderness, the troops were ravaged by hunger and disease. After they met up with another American force, led by General

Richard Montgomery, the combined and exhausted armies made an assault on Quebec on New Year's Eve 1775. It ended in total defeat. Arnold was badly wounded; Montgomery was killed.

As 1776 began, Washington badly needed a ray of hope. The British knew that with soldier enlistments concluding at year's end, Washington's army was melting away. When the Americans greeted the new year by hoisting their newly adopted Grand Union flag, the British thought at first it was a flag of surrender. But in mid-January, American colonel Henry Knox arrived at camp with miraculous news. The previous May, Benedict Arnold and Ethan Allen had taken Fort Ticonderoga in New York, a British frontier post 300 miles northwest of Boston. Knox had engineered the transport—by sled!—of almost 60 mortars and cannons from the fort. Washington finally had the artillery to mount a proper assault. In March 1776, under cover of nightfall, he had the guns mounted on Dorchester Heights, overlooking Boston. When the British awoke to find themselves within firing range, they opted to flee rather than fight. Within a few days, they had boarded ships and sailed out of Boston Harbor for Halifax, Nova Scotia. It was not the decisive battle Washington had been hoping for. But he would very soon get it.

The British had decided to seize control of the Hudson River,

A MAP FROM 1776 SHOWS THE BOSTON AREA DURING THE SIEGE OF BRITISH FORCES. AMERICAN GUNS PLACED AT DORCHESTER HEIGHTS PERSUADED THE BRITISH TO FLEE.

which runs north from New York Harbor toward Canada. If the British could take over the river, it would separate New England from the rest of the colonies, making it difficult to send supplies and communications by land. Determined to foil the British plan, Washington moved his army south toward New York City in April. There, it would be joined by battalions from other colonies. His plan was to confront British forces that were assembling there under the command of General William Howe and Howe's older brother, Admiral Richard Howe.

What Washington did not know was how huge those forces would be. The British were sending 33,000 soldiers and seamen to

America, the largest expeditionary force in their history. By early July 1776, even as the Continental Congress was approving the Declaration of Independence, British fighting men and German mercenaries were pouring into Staten Island, New York, where more than 100 British ships had anchored.

In August, Washington made a very ill-judged decision: he divided his much smaller force between Manhattan (then called York Island) and areas of Long Island, just across the East River. In the battle that began on August 27, his Long Island army was utterly defeated. Two nights later, under cover of darkness, some 9,000 men from the Long Island army made a daring escape by ferry from Brooklyn Heights to Manhattan. For two weeks, Washington and his men occupied New York City, which in those days was confined largely to the southern tip of Manhattan. But in mid-September, they evacuated and the British moved in—only to watch a quarter of the city burn a few days later in a mysterious fire. The British suspected the fire was arson carried out by Washington's agents.

In November, the British defeated the Americans again, this time at Fort Washington in northern Manhattan.

AFTER THE AMERICAN DEFEAT AT THE BATTLE OF LONG ISLAND, WASHINGTON DIRECTED THE NIGHTTIME EVACUATION OF HIS MEN FROM BROOKLYN TO MANHATTAN.

The British took more than 2,800 prisoners and seized valuable artillery and supplies. Just three nights later, General Howe sent 3,000 British soldiers and Hessians (German soldiers paid by the British) under the leadership of General Charles Cornwallis across the Hudson, up the steep cliffs of the New Jersey Palisades, and then toward the American post at Fort Lee. Washington arrived just in time to evacuate about 3,000 of his men and lead them in a miserable retreat across New Jersey. That limping remnant of his army was spared only because Howe ordered Cornwallis to give up the chase, allowing Washington time to get his men across the Delaware River and to Pennsylvania.

THE AMERICANS FELT DEFEATED. THEN WASHINGTON CAME UP WITH ANOTHER PLAN.

The revolutionary forces were in terrible shape, and it seemed likely that the war had been lost. The Americans felt defeated. But then Washington came up with another plan.

General Howe had set up a British camp outside Trenton, New Jersey. On Christmas Eve 1776, while the British were warm in their beds, Washington loaded 2,400 American troops and 18 pieces of artillery onto boats and crossed back over the freezing Delaware River. His soldiers swarmed the Hessians defending the post, killing or wounding about 100 and capturing 900. A week later, they defeated another British force at Princeton. After the terrible losses in New York, those two New Jersey victories helped turn the tide. Once again, the Americans believed they could win.

Martha, My Dear

When she married George Washington, Martha Dandridge Custis was one of the richest women in Virginia. But she brought to her second marriage more than money. Throughout Washington's tumultuous career, she would be his refuge and companion. (She liked to call him her "Old Man.")

CHARLES WILLSON PEALE PAINTED THIS MINIATURE OF MARTHA AROUND 1776.

They were a funny pair. He was over 6 feet tall. She was somewhere around 5 feet. His hands were immense. Hers were tiny. But there was an iron constitution in her little frame. Though she dressed stylishly and was accustomed to comfort, Martha was not afraid of hardship. During the war, she joined her husband every year at the Continental Army's winter quarters, even for the terrible months at Valley Forge. Charming and sociable, she gave him a semblance of normalcy during the nearly eight years the war kept him away from home. And whatever the difficulties of camp life, she was, as she put it, "determined to be cheerful and to be happy in whatever situation."

As the nation's first First Lady—a term that would not come into use until the mid-19th century—she was conscientious in performing her public duties, though she took no great pleasure in carrying them out. It was home life, especially at Mount Vernon, that gave her the most satisfaction.

We know almost nothing of what she and her husband said to each other in letters. Before her death, Martha burned almost their entire personal correspondence. But perhaps Washington told us all we need to know when he said that his marriage to Martha was the event in his life "most conducive to happiness."

PAINTER EMANUEL LEUTZE'S FAMOUS DEPICTION OF WASHINGTON CROSSING THE DELAWARE RIVER WAS COMPLETED IN 1851, 75 YEARS AFTER THE EVENT.

WASHINGTON WAS UNLIKELY TO HAVE STOOD UP DURING A DANGEROUS CROSSING IN ICY WATERS. LEUTZE ROMANTICIZED HIS SUBJECT.

Friends from Abroad

The American cause attracted many European adventurers, who flocked to Washington seeking commissions as high officers in the Continental Army. Most he considered nuisances, but a few became valued comrades. None ranked higher in his affections than Gilbert du Motier, marquis de Lafayette. Orphaned at 12, Lafayette had come into a huge inheritance and mixed freely with King Louis XVI of France and his court at Versailles, but he found aristocratic life unfulfilling. Inspired by the ideals of the American Revolution, in April 1777, the 19-year-old marquis bid farewell to his wife and set sail for America, armed with a letter of introduction from Benjamin Franklin.

Washington would discover that Lafayette—who later named his son Georges Washington—was a valuable soldier and friend. More than that, for the childless general he became a surrogate son. A brave and resourceful officer, Lafayette shared the hardships of Valley Forge without complaint and fought valiantly in numerous battles. After the war, he also helped move Washington to an understanding that slavery was wrong and must end.

Lafayette was a true aristocrat. The other notable foreign addition to Washington's officer corps was no such thing. "Baron" Friedrich von Steuben, also sent to America by Franklin, had given himself his noble title. Even the rank he claimed to Washington—lieutenant general—was invented by Franklin to make Steuben seem more qualified; he had never risen above captain.

But Steuben's military skills were genuine. In February 1778, the onetime staff officer for Frederick the Great turned up (with his greyhound) at Valley Forge. Well schooled in Prussian military discipline, he soon set to work instructing the amateurish Americans in the fundamentals of European military discipline. It was Steuben who showed them how to use bayonets and how to march like soldiers. He drilled the men daily, teaching them to fall into the columns and lines essential to battlefield maneuvers. Soon he had written *Regulations for the Order and Discipline of the Troops of the United States*, a drill manual that remained in use until the Civil War.

Another big step for the Americans happened in December 1776: more than 3,000 miles away, Benjamin Franklin arrived in Paris. The Americans had been receiving secret shipments of supplies from the French, and Franklin had been sent to try to persuade them to openly support the American cause.

Once again, the one-year enlistments of Washington's men were expiring, and the army dwindled to no more than 3,000. By now, Washington had decided that he could no longer risk direct attacks on British forces. For the rest of the war, his troops would harass the British when it was possible but retreat whenever they were at risk. In January 1777, Washington took an unusual step to protect his men: he had them inoculated against smallpox. The potentially deadly disease could sweep through the tight, often

THE MARQUIS DE LAFAYETTE BECAME A LIFELONG FRIEND OF GEORGE WASHINGTON.

dirty quarters that troops shared. Washington's earlier exposure to smallpox had spared him from getting it again, but a large outbreak could destroy an army. Some historians think that Washington's decision to vaccinate the troops was as important as any military moves he made.

In March, Washington made another decision that would prove to be significant for the development of the country.

He appointed a young soldier named Alexander Hamilton to be his aide-de-camp.

In the early autumn of 1777, the Americans lost two more battles, at Brandywine and Germantown, Pennsylvania. But in October came astounding news. At Saratoga, outside Albany, New York, American troops commanded by General Horatio Gates had joined with New England militias to overwhelm a large British force under General John Burgoyne. About 6,000 British soldiers surrendered.

This great victory, a turning point in the war, had one really big effect. Convinced at last that the American dream of breaking away from Britain was attainable, France officially entered the war on the American side in February 1778. This was what Benjamin Franklin had spent more than a year in Paris trying to achieve. Britain would now face a formidable alliance, not just a ragtag group of fighters.

But before the French could help them, the Americans first had to survive a bitter winter. Washington and his men huddled miserably at Valley Forge, Pennsylvania, through the winter of 1777 to 1778. Camped on a windy plateau 20 miles northwest of Philadelphia, the ragged soldiers were short of clothing, blankets, and food. Some even lacked shoes. As they first approached the place in December, they left bloody footprints in the snow. Most spent the first months of the winter in flimsy tents. States did not want to levy taxes to finance the war, and the Continental Congress was nearly bankrupt. The Congress urged Washington to seize food and supplies from the surrounding farms, but Washington refused. As freezing temperatures settled in and illness swept the camp, conditions became unbearable. A doctor there described it this way: "Poor food—hard lodging—cold weather—fatigue—nasty clothes—nasty cookery . . . I can't endure it." Washington warned the Congress that without more food, the army would "starve, dissolve, or disperse."

Remarkably, they did none of those during that awful winter. That there was no mutiny was due in good measure to the near-religious reverence that Washington commanded.

THAT THERE WAS NO MUTINY WAS DUE IN GOOD MEASURE TO THE NEAR-RELIGIOUS REVERENCE THAT WASHINGTON COMMANDED.

The admiration of his troops would help Washington through another threat that winter. After Gates's triumph at Saratoga, a victory in which Washington played no part, some critics began to publicly question Washington's leadership. They started a whispering campaign to try to have him removed from his command. They sent letters to members of the Continental Congress. When Gates returned to Philadelphia after the victory at Saratoga, he should have reported to Washington, his commanding officer. Instead, Gates delivered his report to the Continental Congress.

At the forefront of the anti-Washington campaign was Brigadier General Thomas Conway, one of the many foreign adventurers who had joined the Continental Army. Conway, who was angry that

MY BRAVE FELLOWS, YOU HAVE DONE ALL I ASKED YOU TO DO, A MORE THAN CAN BE REASONAB EXPECTED; BUT YOUR COUNTRY IS STAKE, YOUR WIVES, YOUR HOUS AND ALL THAT YOU HOLD DEAR

AT VALLEY FORGE, THE ARMY FACED BITTER COLD, ILLNESS, AND INSUFFICIEN FOOD.

Washington had refused to promote him to major general, stirred up doubts among members of the Congress about Washington's abilities. He even got the Congress to award him the promotion his commander had opposed. But Washington's reputation protected him from the schemes being hatched against him. By April 1778, Conway had been forced from the army, and in July of that year, he was wounded in a duel with a Washington supporter.

In the spring of 1778, things began to look up for Washington and his army. Even amid the sufferings of Valley Forge, they had been training with Baron von Steuben. And by the time the Continental Army marched out in June, new enlistments had swelled its numbers to about 12,000. By then, London had replaced General Howe with General Sir Henry Clinton, who moved his forces out of Philadelphia and back toward New York. En route, his men encountered the now well-drilled Americans, who more than held their own at the Battle of Monmouth in New Jersey.

The French, having declared war on Britain, sent a fleet across the Atlantic that anchored off Delaware Bay on July 8, 1778. Washington hoped it would quickly be made available to him for a combined land and sea assault against the main British force, ideally in New York. But following a failed mission in Newport, Rhode Island, the French admiral—Charles-Hector, count d'Estaing—sailed his fleet to the Caribbean to protect French interests there against the British.

Washington spent part of the next year directing a campaign against the Iroquois Confederacy, also known as the Six Nations. Recognizing that the British were far more willing than the Americans to protect native lands from white incursion, four of the six Iroquois nations sided with Britain in the war. They launched raids against frontier settlements in upstate New York and western Pennsylvania. In June 1779, Washington sent 4,000 men under General John Sullivan into the region to achieve, as he wrote to Sullivan, "the total destruction and devastation" of Iroquois villages. Dozens would be burned to the ground, a blow from which the Iroquois Confederacy never entirely recovered.

COUNT DE ROCHAMBEAU COMMANDED THE ARMY SENT BY FRANCE TO ASSIST THE AMERICANS, THOUGH HE WAS IN NO HURRY TO PUT IT TO USE.

Even as Sullivan was pursuing the Iroquois, the British were launching a sizable campaign in the Carolinas. On May 12, 1780, the British seized Charleston, South Carolina, along with almost 2,600 American soldiers. It was a devastating loss for the Americans and put the British in a position to launch attacks all across the lightly defended South. After Charleston fell, General Gates, the victor at Saratoga, was appointed to command the southern army. But in August, Gates was defeated by the British at Camden, South Carolina. Worse, he fled the battlefield on horseback, an embarrassment that led the Continental Congress to relieve him of his command. Washington at least had the satisfaction of seeing Gates disgraced.

Then, in September, Washington suffered a huge betrayal. That month, he traveled to the Hudson River fort at West Point, New York, to confer with one of his most trusted and enterprising officers, Major General Benedict Arnold. Arnold had led the attack on Quebec at the beginning of the war and had fought with honor at the Battle of Saratoga. What Washington did not know was that Arnold, who considered himself inadequately rewarded for having won important battles in which he had sustained lasting injuries, had made a deal with a British officer, Major John André. In exchange for money and a commission in His Majesty's Army, the treacherous Arnold had agreed to deliver the fort at West Point to the British.

Sited on a bluff over the Hudson River, the fort was essential in keeping the British from taking the river and completing their plan to cut off the land route between New England and the southern states. Losing it would likely mean defeat for the Americans. Luckily, just days before Washington departed for West Point, André was arrested carrying papers from Arnold that revealed the plot. Alerted to the arrest, Arnold escaped to the protection of the British. André was convicted of spying and hanged. Arnold joined the British Army, led raids on coastal towns in Virginia and Connecticut, and later relocated to England with his wife.

ALL HIS LIFE, WASHINGTON WOULD BE HAUNTED BY ARNOLD'S BETRAYAL.

All his life, Washington would be aggrieved by Arnold's betrayal.

Benedict Arnold was hardly the only soldier to mutiny. As the year 1781 dawned, Washington saw one of his greatest fears realized. For years, he had pleaded with the

Congress to provide his men with adequate food, supplies, and pay—or any pay at all. On New Year's Day, more than a thousand Pennsylvania troops (who had not been paid in over a year) mutinied, killing several officers. Armed with muskets and cannons, they headed for Philadelphia with the intent of pressuring the Congress. The mutineers were halted before they reached the city and their leaders executed by firing squad. Some days later, so were the leaders of a second mutinous unit, this one from New Jersey.

Arnold's treachery and the two mutinies made Washington wonder if his army was finally disintegrating. But that same year, the French decided to send another fleet across the Atlantic. With the states still unable to raise revenue, the French also agreed to a large loan and a gift of cash for arms and supplies.

So it was that in the autumn of 1781, Washington's fortunes—and his nation's—turned around completely. All that summer, Britain's General Cornwallis had been conducting campaigns in Virginia in the hope of luring Washington into a major battle there. Washington did not take the bait until he got word that the French fleet—28 ships carrying 3,500 troops—was on its way from the West Indies. When the battle finally began, at Yorktown, Virginia, in October, 9,000 French soldiers marched alongside 10,000 Americans and cornered the enemy. French ships clogged the mouth of the Chesapeake Bay, preventing a British naval rescue. For days, American and French cannon fire decimated the British ranks. On October 19, 1781, Cornwallis formally surrendered. The war was over.

Washington did not realize at first that Yorktown was the final battle of the war. But Lord Frederick North, the British prime minister, did. When he got word of the defeat, he shouted, "Oh, God! It is all over!"

Washington was soon distracted from his victory by news that his 26-year-old stepson, Jacky, who had joined him at Yorktown as an aide-de-camp, was dying of "camp fever." Jacky was moved

A PAINTING BASED ON NOTES TAKEN AT THE BATTLE OF YORKTOWN SHOWS FRENCH TROOPS DESCENDING TOWARD BRITISH POSITIONS NEAR THE BANKS OF THE YORK RIVER.

to an uncle's estate, where his mother and wife came to nurse him and where Washington arrived on November 5, just in time to witness his death.

Although the war was over, Washington refused to dissolve the Continental Army before England had signed a peace treaty. Some Americans grew suspicious that he might try to use the army to place himself in power. To make matters worse, a group of officers upset about their payment were indeed hoping that Washington would lead a military takeover of the government. To forestall a planned meeting of the discontented officers in Philadelphia, Washington called his own assembly on March 15, 1783, a year and a half after the surrender at Yorktown. Taking the stage at an auditorium called the Temple of Virtue, he reminded his audience, "It can scarcely be supposed, at this late stage of the war, that I am indifferent to [your] interests." But he asked the officers to reject anyone who "wickedly" attempted to "overturn the liberties of [the] country, and . . . open the floodgates of civil discord, and deluge [the] rising empire in blood."

Washington had proven his devotion to the ideal of democratic rule. The threatened rebellion melted away. (It helped that the Congress soon granted the officers pensions equal to five years' pay.) On September 3, 1783, the peace treaty with Britain was signed. And on December 4, Washington arrived at Fraunces Tavern in New York City, where more than 30 of his officers were gathered to bid him farewell. Then the 51-year-old general, weary and graying, went home again to Mount Vernon. The war really was over. But the turbulent peace was just beginning.

JOHN TRUMBULL'S FAMOUS PAINTING OF THE BRITISH SURRENDER AT
YORKTOWN SHOWS AMERICAN MAJOR GENERAL BENJAMIN LINCOLN
ACCEPTING THE OFFICIAL SURRENDER FROM A DEPUTY OF LORD

CORNWALLIS, WHO DID NOT ATTEND THE CEREMONY. WASHINGTON (ON THE BROWN HORSE AT RIGHT) REFUSED TO ACCEPT THE SURRENDER PERSONALLY FROM ANYONE OTHER THAN CORNWALLIS.

George Washington and Slavery

IN THE WORLD OF VIRGINIA PLANTERS INTO WHICH WASHINGTON WAS BORN, SLAVERY WAS ACCEPTED AS A FACT OF LIFE. IN 1732, THE YEAR OF WASHINGTON'S BIRTH, EVEN MANY NORTHERNERS HAD SLAVES. BENJAMIN FRANKLIN, WHO WOULD LATER BECOME AN ABOLITIONIST, HAD TWO ENSLAVED PEOPLE WITH HIM WHEN HE TRAVELED TO LONDON IN 1757. WHAT IS REMARKABLE ABOUT WASHINGTON IS NOT THAT HE OWNED SLAVES ALL HIS LIFE BUT THAT HE WAS EVENTUALLY ABLE TO RECOGNIZE THAT SLAVERY MUST END.

AN ANNOUNCEMENT FOR A SLAVE AUCTION PUBLISHED IN THE JUNE 23, 1768, ISSUE OF THE *NEW YORK JOURNAL OR GENERAL ADVERTISER.* THE FIRST U.S. CENSUS, IN 1790, COUNTED 681,000 ENSLAVED PEOPLE— ONE-SIXTH OF THE POPULATION OF THE UNITED STATES.

A 19TH-CENTURY IDEALIZATION OF LIFE AT MOUNT VERNON.

A DETAIL FROM A DIAGRAM OF SLAVE QUARTERS ON A BRITISH SLAVE SHIP SHOWS THE INHUMANE CONDITIONS OF THE TRANSATLANTIC PASSAGE.

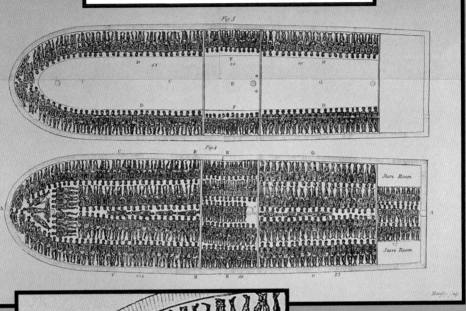

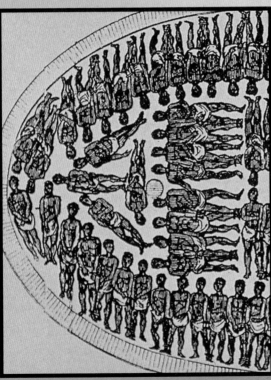

WASHINGTON'S PERSONAL SERVANT, WILLIAM LEE (CALLED BILLY LEE), WAS ONE OF TWO ENSLAVED PEOPLE WASHINGTON BOUGHT AT AUCTION IN 1768. BILLY LEE WENT EVERYWHERE WITH WASHINGTON—ON THE FOXHUNTS HIS MASTER LOVED, THROUGH ALL THE CAMPAIGNS OF THE REVOLUTIONARY WAR, AND THEN TO NEW YORK AND PHILADELPHIA WHEN WASHINGTON BECAME PRESIDENT.

IN HIS YOUNGER YEARS, WASHINGTON THOUGHT NOTHING OF OWNING SLAVES. BETWEEN 1760 AND 1775, WASHINGTON MORE THAN DOUBLED THE NUMBER OF ENSLAVED PEOPLE AT MOUNT VERNON, TO OVER 100. THOSE WHO WERE SKILLED— AS BREWERS, CART MAKERS, BLACKSMITHS, BAKERS, AND SO FORTH—WORKED MOSTLY AT THE FARM CONNECTED TO THE MAIN HOUSE. FIELD WORKERS, MOST OF THEM WOMEN, WERE ASSIGNED TO THE FOUR OUTLYING FARMS.

ABOUT A DOZEN ENSLAVED PEOPLE WORKED INSIDE THE HOUSE ITSELF, WHERE THEY DRESSED IN SCARLET UNIFORMS WITH WHITE WAISTCOATS. THOUGH SLAVERY IS BY ITS VERY NATURE CRUEL, NO EVIDENCE PAINTS WASHINGTON AS A PARTICULARLY HARSH MASTER BY THE STANDARDS OF THE TIME. HE SOLD SLAVES WHEN HE NEEDED TO, BUT HE WOULD NOT BREAK UP FAMILIES. ALL THE SAME, MANY OF HIS ENSLAVED WORKERS RAN AWAY. (DURING THE WAR, 17 RAN OFF WITH THE BRITISH.) AND WHILE HE GREW TO DETEST THE PRACTICE OF WHIPPING, THERE WERE INSTANCES WHEN HE PERMITTED IT, SUCH AS WHEN REPEAT RUNAWAYS WERE CAUGHT.

THIS INVENTORY OF THE ENSLAVED PEOPLE AT MOUNT VERNON WAS DRAWN UP BY WASHINGTON WHEN HE PREPARED HIS WILL.

WHAT CAUSED WASHINGTON TO CHANGE HIS MIND, HOWEVER SLOWLY, ABOUT SLAVERY? IT BEGAN AS A PURE BUSINESS CALCULATION. UNLIKE HIRED LABORERS, ENSLAVED PEOPLE NEEDED TO BE FED, CLOTHED, AND HOUSED, EVEN WHEN THEY WERE TOO YOUNG, TOO OLD, OR TOO SICK TO WORK. THEN, DURING THE REVOLUTIONARY WAR, WASHINGTON WAS EXPOSED TO A WIDER RANGE OF VIEWS ON SLAVERY THAN HE HAD ENCOUNTERED IN VIRGINIA. AND THEN THERE WAS THE REVOLUTION ITSELF. THE REVOLUTION'S IDEALS OF LIBERTY AND EQUALITY WERE IMPOSSIBLE TO RECONCILE WITH A SYSTEM OF HUMAN BONDAGE. ANY NUMBER OF SLAVE OWNERS WENT TO WAR UNTROUBLED BY THE CONTRADICTION. BUT AS COMMANDER AND THEN AS PRESIDENT, WASHINGTON KNEW THAT MORE WAS DEMANDED OF HIM.

AN ENGRAVING DEPICTS MARTHA WASHINGTON (IN BLUE) KNITTING WHILE AN ENSLAVED WOMAN CUTS CLOTH.

DOMESTIC LIFE AT MOUNT VERNON.

DURING HIS LIFE, WASHINGTON NEVER FREED HIS SLAVES, THOUGH HE SOMETIMES SPOKE OF DOING IT. AND THROUGHOUT HIS PRESIDENCY, HE TOOK NO STEPS TO RAISE THE ISSUE, FEARING IT WOULD PUSH THE SOUTH OUT OF THE UNION. ONLY AT HIS DEATH, WHEN HE DIRECTED THAT HIS SLAVES SHOULD BE FREED AFTER THE DEATH OF HIS WIFE, DID HE AT LAST PROMISE THEM FREEDOM.

A BUMPY ROAD

3

In which a battle-weary general retires once more, the new country suffers growing pains, and a plan for the future is forged.

On Christmas Eve 1783, Washington arrived back at Mount Vernon. During the war, he had feared that British raiders might burn Mount Vernon. Instead, it was the neighboring Fairfax estate, the scene of so many happy memories of his youth, that had suffered a serious fire. Still, Mount Vernon had fallen into disrepair while he was gone. Just as he had after the French and Indian War, Washington threw himself into improving his beloved estate. He restored fields, bred mules, and worked to solve

1783
RETIRED
AGAIN TO
MOUNT VERNON

1786
START OF
SHAYS'S
REBELLION

AFTER THE WAR, MANY ARTISTS BEAT A PATH TO WASHINGTON'S DOOR. IN 1785, THE GREAT SCULPTOR JEAN-ANTOINE HOUDON TRAVELED FROM FRANCE TO MAKE THIS TERRA-COTTA BUST.

1787
ELECTED
PRESIDENT OF
CONSTITUTIONAL
CONVENTION

1789
ELECTED
PRESIDENT
OF THE UNITED
STATES

IN 1784, THE MARQUIS DE LAFAYETTE (IN RED) VISITED WASHINGTON AT MOUNT VERNON.

the estate's money problems. Mount Vernon was making less and less money, and Washington earned income mainly from rental fees, which flowed from the 30,000 acres of western land he had been wise enough to acquire early.

Washington wanted to return to the quiet life of a country gentleman, but that proved difficult to do. He had gained fame over the previous eight years and was now probably the most revered

man in America. A steady stream of visitors came to his door. Painters and sculptors showed up frequently to make likenesses of the famous general. Washington would have to sit for hours while the artists worked. He found it tiresome, but he knew that their work would preserve his memory. As he explained in a letter to the marquis de Lafayette, artists were the "doorkeepers to the temple of fame."

The years after his return from the war were largely happy ones. But at the same time, it was clear the general was feeling his age. He was 51 when he came home, and feeling wintry. His father and brothers had all died young, and it was clear that Washington thought his own life had likely come close to its end. In another letter to Lafayette, Washington wrote that he "might soon expect to be entombed in the dreary mansions of [his] father's." But Washington's part in history was not finished yet. The new United States was suffering growing pains.

Before the end of the Revolutionary War, the 13 fledgling states had signed the Articles of Confederation, a set of rules by which the new nation would be governed. In many ways, the articles had declared a nation without truly creating one. After fighting for freedom from a monarchy, Americans were wary about giving too much power to a central government. So the articles created a government with no president or supreme court, just a Congress in which each state had an equal vote and important measures required the consent of at least nine states. The Congress had no power to regulate trade. It could not impose taxes without the unanimous agreement of all the states. And it had no power to force states to carry out its directives.

No one was more aware of the dangers of a weak government than Washington. During the war, he had pleaded with the Continental Congress over and over for the money to supply and pay his troops. When the war ended, he was appalled to learn that, though veterans had been promised in 1780 a pension of half pay for life, the Congress had not raised the money to provide it.

The articles would have caused problems in the best of times. In the uncertain time that followed the war, they were a formula for disaster. After the war, the country fell into an economic depression that only grew worse until 1786. Prices, wages, and employment rates fell. As bankruptcies and foreclosures spread, farmers and small business owners were jammed into prisons for not paying their debts.

While the Congress argued over how to create a national currency, people used all kinds of money, including British shillings, Spanish pistoles and doubloons, and French crowns. Individual states printed their own money and forced businesses to accept the cash as payment for debts. But the new money quickly lost value, leading many merchants to flee from debtors so as not to have potentially worthless notes forced on them.

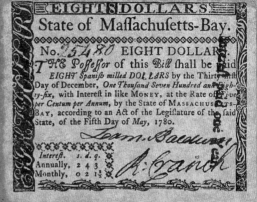

UNDER THE ARTICLES OF CONFEDERATION, CURRENCIES OF MANY KINDS CIRCULATED IN THE U.S. ABOVE, A VIRGINIA BANKNOTE. AT RIGHT, ONE FROM MASSACHUSETTS.

The Congress could not even raise enough cash to make interest payments on the $54 million war debt. And getting states to contribute proved tricky. In 1782 and 1783, the Congress got just $1.5 million of the $10 million it asked the states to contribute for government expenses. "Our pretended union is but a name," the Connecticut patriot Noah Webster lamented, "our confederation, a cobweb."

Hard times were made harder when states tried to raise money at the expense of their neighbors. New York taxed firewood from Connecticut and vegetables from New Jersey. In the sparsely settled western territories, multiple states claimed the same lands. The weak government also caused problems in foreign relations. Knowing that the feeble Congress could do nothing to stop them, British troops held on to several forts in the Northwest that they had promised, in the peace treaty following the war, to leave.

In the spring of 1786, Secretary of Foreign Affairs John Jay reported to Washington that a movement was afoot to change the hopeless Articles of Confederation. Washington was pleased by the news but felt that it would take a crisis to move the states to take any real action. The crisis came soon enough. That autumn, thousands of debt-ridden Massachusetts farmers joined a rebellion led by a former militia captain named Daniel Shays. Armed with guns and pitchforks, they intimidated judges and shut down courts to prevent the start of bankruptcy proceedings against them.

As it happened, representatives from five states were meeting in September 1786 to try to settle disputes between states. They realized that the only way to solve their problems was to amend, or change, the articles. They issued a call, written by Alexander Hamilton, for each state to send representatives to a meeting in Philadelphia the following May. When Washington got word of the announcement, he was greatly pleased. Very soon, James Madison and James Monroe were at Mount Vernon to try to get his support for reform. "Shays's Rebellion," which would drag on until February 1787, only strengthened Washington's resolve that action was needed.

By that time, Washington had already been told that the Virginia legislature planned to name him head of the state's seven-man delegation to the meeting in Philadelphia. At first he resisted. He feared that the gathering would damage his reputation if it failed to make any meaningful change to the articles. But by spring he had been won over. (Martha, on the other hand, was deeply unhappy about his return to public life and would not go with him.) On May 13, 1787, Washington was escorted into Philadelphia by a parade

THE UNITED STATES, AND NEIGHBORING TERRITORIES CLAIMED BY BRITAIN AND SPAIN, AS THEY APPEARED IN 1784.

of dignitaries and mounted soldiers that made its way through cheering crowds. As everyone expected, when the Constitutional Convention was called into session two weeks later, he was the unanimous choice to become its president.

Though they had been instructed by the Congress to do no more than amend the Articles of Confederation, the delegates set out from the first to produce an entirely new charter of government—the U.S. Constitution. In his role as president, Washington was expected to stay out of the debates about the new document, which suited him. He knew he wanted a stronger central government, but for the details of its construction, he looked to John Jay and James Madison. They were the ones who sketched out what came to be called the Virginia Plan—a three-part structure of government consisting

SIGNING OF THE U.S. CONSTITUTION, 1787 HOWARD CHANDLER CHRISTY'S 1940 PAINTING SHOWS ALL 39 SIGNERS, AS WELL AS WILLIAM JACKSON (IN RED AT CENTER), SECRETARY OF THE CONVENTION.

❶ JOHN RUTLEDGE A DELEGAT FROM SOUTH CAROLINA, HE CHAIRE THE COMMITTEE OF DETAIL, WHICH DREW UP A FIRST DRAFT OF THE CONSTITUTION BASED ON 19 RESOLUTIONS ADOPTED EARLIER IN THE CONVENTION.

❹ ALEXANDER HAMILTON AFTER THE SIGNING OF THE CONSTITUTION, HE, JAMES MADISON, AND JOHN JAY WOULD WRITE THE FAMOUS SERIES OF ARTICLES THAT BECAME *THE FEDERALIST*.

❺ BENJAMIN FRANKLIN OTHER THAN GEORGE WASHINGTON, BENJAMIN FRANKLIN WAS THE MOST EMINENT FIGURE AT THE CONVENTION. AT 81, HE WAS ALSO THE OLDEST. HE SAID LITTLE DURING DELIBERATIONS.

❷ GOUVERNEUR MORRIS A NEW YORKER IN THE PENNSYLVANIA DELEGATION, HE WAS A STRONG OPPONENT OF SLAVERY. HE WAS APPOINTED BY THE CONVENTION TO PRODUCE THE FINAL DRAFT OF THE CONSTITUTION. ITS LANGUAGE IS LARGELY HIS.

❸ GEORGE WASHINGTON WASHINGTON SAID LITTLE THROUGHOUT THE CONVENTION. ALTHOUGH HE WAS STRONGLY IN FAVOR OF A MORE POWERFUL CENTRAL GOVERNMENT, HE FELT THAT HIS ROLE AS PRESIDING OFFICER REQUIRED HIM TO STAY OUT OF DEBATES.

❻ JAMES MADISON ONE OF THE KEY ARCHITECTS OF THE CONSTITUTION, MADISON ALSO KEPT METICULOUS NOTES, WHICH PROVIDED FUTURE GENERATIONS WITH DETAILED ACCOUNTS OF THE CONVENTION'S DEBATES.

❼ JAMES WILSON A PENNSYLVANIAN, HE DRAFTED A KEY COMPROMISE WITH SOUTHERN STATES. IT COUNTED ENSLAVED PEOPLE AS THREE-FIFTHS OF A PERSON WHEN DETERMINING A STATE'S POPULATION, AND THUS THE SIZE OF ITS CONGRESSIONAL DELEGATION.

of an executive, a two-chamber legislature with representation proportional to state population, and a judiciary. The smaller states argued against proportional representation, since it would leave them with fewer representatives. As the debates grew more contentious, Washington remained impartial (although he secretly agreed with Madison). In the end, the smaller and larger states compromised. The number of representatives a state could send to the House of Representatives would depend on its population. In the Senate, each state would have an equal number of senators: two.

The convention also debated how the executive branch should be formed. Some delegates feared that a president might become a tyrant. They wanted an executive council made up of three leaders. The fact that the convention eventually opted for a single president—who even had power to veto acts of the legislature— probably had a lot to do with the widespread faith that Washington (whom nearly everyone assumed would be the first president) would set a standard for the careful use of power. As one delegate later put it, the convention would probably not have created such a powerful presidency "had not many members cast their eyes toward General Washington."

A third issue that caused a lot of argument was slavery. Southern delegations threatened to walk out if the Constitution interfered with slavery. Eventually the delegates came to a compromise. They did not mention the word *slavery* directly in the text, and they agreed to count each enslaved person as three-fifths of a person for the purposes of determining the population of a state.

The Constitutional Convention ended on September 17, 1787. Though Washington was disappointed in some details of the new Constitution—he was sorry it wasn't clearer about how the three branches would relate to one another—he strongly supported it and was the first to sign it. By June of the following year, it had been ratified by nine states. Two more would sign on soon after. The only thing that remained was to choose a president.

While many assumed he would be president, Washington was careful not to appear to be pursuing the job. But with the persistent urging of Hamilton and other supporters, he allowed himself to be persuaded. There was no real opponent, and since the Congress had decided that electors chosen in January 1789 would cast their votes just a few weeks later, there was no campaign season, no need to deliver speeches or take part in debates. In the end, George Washington was the one person who best represented the ideals of the revolution. On February 4, 1789, Washington won the entire electoral vote, with 69 ballots. He remains the only president to be elected unanimously. In the more contentious contest for the vice presidency, John Adams was the winner, with 34 votes against 9 for John Jay.

Officially informed of the result in April—though he was already well aware of it—Washington at last acknowledged that the unanimous vote "scarcely [left him] the alternative for an option."

Washington was headed to the nation's capital, then New York City, to become the first president of the United States of America.

WASHINGTON REMAINS THE ONLY PRESIDENT TO BE ELECTED UNANIMOUSLY.

A Frightening Insurrection

AN ILLUSTRATION FROM 1786 SHOWS A BLACKSMITH BEING GIVEN A WRIT OF ATTACHMENT—AN ORDER TO SEIZE THE ASSETS OF A DEBTOR—DURING SHAYS'S REBELLION.

NO EVENT DID SO MUCH TO CONVINCE AMERICANS THAT THEY NEEDED A MORE EFFECTIVE NATIONAL GOVERNMENT AS THE ARMED REVOLT CALLED SHAYS'S REBELLION. IN THE YEARS THAT FOLLOWED THE END OF THE REVOLUTIONARY WAR, FARMERS IN MANY PARTS OF THE COUNTRY FOUND THEMSELVES DROWNING IN DEBT. NEGLECTED ARMY VETERANS GREW FRUSTRATED, TOO. DURING THE WAR, THEY HAD BEEN PAID IN CONTINENTAL SCRIP, A FORM OF MONEY THAT SOON LOST ALMOST ALL ITS VALUE. WASHINGTON RECEIVED LETTERS FROM HIS FORMER OFFICERS THAT WERE FILLED WITH SENTIMENT IN FAVOR OF A MILITARY GOVERNMENT OR EVEN CROWNING A KING.

STARTING IN THE SUMMER AND FALL OF 1786, DEBT-RIDDEN FARMERS, LED BY AN ARMY VETERAN NAMED DANIEL SHAYS, TRIED TO STOP BANKRUPTCY PROCEEDINGS BY PREVENTING COURTS FROM CONVENING IN SEVERAL TOWNS IN WESTERN MASSACHUSETTS. LOCAL MILITIA REFUSED TO STOP THE REBELS AND SOMETIMES EVEN JOINED THEM. THE CONGRESS LACKED THE MONEY TO RAISE TROOPS TO PUT DOWN THE DISORDER, AND PANICKY MERCHANTS IN BOSTON HAD TO FINANCE THEIR OWN MILITIA OF 4,000 MEN FOR PROTECTION.

REBELLIOUS FARMERS LED BY DANIEL SHAYS MAKE THEIR DOOMED APPROACH TO THE ARSENAL AT SPRINGFIELD, MASSACHUSETTTS

IN LATE JANUARY 1787, AS THE REVOLT GATHERED STEAM, THE REBELS MARCHED ON THE CONTINENTAL ARMY ARSENAL AT SPRINGFIELD, MASSACHUSETTS. THEY WERE MET BY THE NEW MILITIA AND OTHER STATE TROOPS UNDER THE COMMAND OF WILLIAM SHEPARD. THE STATE FORCES FIRED CANNONS INTO THE REBEL RANKS, KILLING SEVERAL MEN AND SCATTERING THE REST. IN THE WEEK THAT FOLLOWED, SHAYS AND HIS MEN WERE PURSUED THROUGH THE BERKSHIRE MOUNTAINS. SURPRISED BY SHEPARD'S FORCES IN THE TOWN OF PETERSHAM, MASSACHUSETTS, THE REBELS RETREATED INTO THE COUNTRYSIDE AGAIN. MOST SIMPLY WENT HOME. THOUGH SOME LEADERS OF THE REBELLION WOULD BE TRIED AND SENTENCED TO DEATH, MOST WERE LATER PARDONED.

DANIEL SHAYS

In which Mr. Washington assumes the presidency and finds that it is not to his liking at all.

It took Washington eight days to make the journey from Mount Vernon to New York City. His inauguration was scheduled to take place there on April 30, 1789. The trip might have gone more quickly, but at every town of any size, there was a ceremony to greet him. At one stop, young girls in white scattered petals in his path. At another, an angelic little boy was lowered from above to place a laurel wreath on his brow. In New York, a presidential barge carried him the final miles, with a flotilla trailing behind it.

1789
INAUGURATED
AT FEDERAL
HALL, NY

1790
SIGNED
TREATY WITH
CREEK NATION

20TH-CENTURY PAINTING IMAGINES THE TUMULT AS WASHINGTON ARRIVED IN NEW YORK CITY ON APRIL 23, 1789.

A huge crowd turned out to greet him when he arrived.

Washington made it a point not to wear his general's uniform. He did not want to fuel any worries that he would lead a military government. He took the oath of office on the balcony of Federal Hall in lower Manhattan, where the newly renamed United States Congress met. Then he created a tradition by walking into the hall and speaking to Congress in the first inaugural address. His short speech emphasized the need for Americans to think of themselves as a nation, not a loose fabric of "local prejudices."

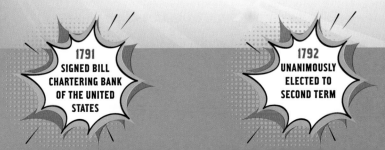

1791
SIGNED BILL
CHARTERING BANK
OF THE UNITED
STATES

1792
UNANIMOUSLY
ELECTED TO
SECOND TERM

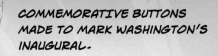

Unity would be the constant theme of Washington's presidency. Determined to see the former colonies join together as a single nation, he struggled to avoid partisan squabbles. Yet as president he had to pursue specific policies, some of them sure to arouse opposition. The drafters of the Constitution had left many of the powers of each branch of government deliberately ill defined, expecting them to be worked out in practice over time. So it would fall to Washington, as the first chief executive, to work out the details. And he did—in his first term, he persuaded the Senate that its power to approve presidential appointees did not include the power to prevent the president from dismissing disappointing cabinet members. By deciding to deliver a speech every year to both houses of Congress, Washington created the State of the Union address. He memorably said, "I walk on untrodden ground," meaning that no one had ever before tried to do what he was doing. But he was determined to go forward boldly. "No fear of encountering difficulties and no dread of losing popularity," he promised, "shall ever deter me from pursuing what I conceive to be the true interests of my country."

WASHINGTON TOOK THE OATH OF OFFICE AT NEW YORK'S FEDERAL HALL.

As the government struggled to find its way, conflicts appeared. Three members of Washington's inner circle were among the sharpest minds of the age. One of them was James Madison, a chief architect of the Constitution and Bill of Rights and, by 1789, a leading member of the House of Representatives. Another was Alexander Hamilton, an aide-de-camp to Washington during the war and now, as his secretary of the treasury, principal champion of the idea of a powerful federal government. As time went on, Hamilton and Madison would split bitterly over issues of federal power. Madison's equal and ally in those fights was

JAMES MADISON, AN ARCHITECT OF THE CONSTITUTION, FOUGHT ATTEMPTS TO EXPAND FEDERAL POWER.

ALEXANDER HAMILTON, WASHINGTON'S TIRELESS TREASURY SECRETARY, CHAMPIONED A VIGOROUS FEDERAL ROLE IN THE ECONOMY.

the third member of the trio, Washington's secretary of state, Thomas Jefferson.

The three men disagreed on the best way to solve the country's biggest problem: debt. War debt still loomed over the new nation. In the fall of 1789, Congress asked Hamilton to come up with a way to settle the debt. In January 1790, he came back with a report on public credit. He proposed combining the debt owed by the federal government with all the debt belonging to the states—about $77 million altogether. When a state or the federal

THE WHOLE ART OF GOVERNMENT CONSISTS IN THE ART OF BEING HONEST.

SECRETARY OF STATE THOMAS JEFFERSON SHARED MADISON'S FEAR OF "MONARCHICAL" CENTRAL POWER.

government borrowed money during the war, the borrower would issue a promissory note—a letter promising to repay the debt—to the lender. Hamilton wanted to allow debt holders to exchange their old promissory notes for new federal securities. The government would promise to set aside tax revenues each year to pay off the debts—but no more than 2% in any year.

Hamilton's plan assumed that the federal government had the power to guide the economy. To Americans wary of federal power of any kind, that was a problem. Southerners also suspected that Hamilton's scheme favored northern states, where the centers of finance were located. Madison, a Virginian, was a ferocious leader of the opposition to Hamilton's plan.

In June, when the House agreed to most of Hamilton's funding scheme, it did not approve one of its central elements: his plan to have the federal government assume state-issued debt. States like Virginia, Maryland, and Georgia, which had repaid most of their wartime debt, objected that they would have to help pay the obligations of the other states. And anyone worried about federal power recognized that by taking over the state debt—and with it the right to collect taxes to repay that debt—the central government would become more powerful. That was indeed one of Hamilton's motives.

The problem was resolved in an unusual way. Hamilton, Madison, and Jefferson met for a private dinner. Jefferson was also against Hamilton's vision of a strong central government but could not say so in public because he was part of Washington's cabinet. At the dinner, Madison and Jefferson made a surprising offer. Efforts to choose a location for the nation's capital had stalled in Congress. Legislators could not agree whether it should remain in New York, move to Philadelphia, or be located on an undeveloped site on the Potomac. As Virginians, Jefferson and Madison wanted the capital on the Potomac. They promised to help pass a bill in Congress that allowed the federal government to take over states' debt—if Hamilton agreed to talk northern congressional delegations into supporting moving the capital to the Potomac. Hamilton badly wanted New York to become the permanent capital, but he wanted his bill more. A few weeks after that dinner, Congress did indeed opt for the Potomac. In the meantime, it was decided, Congress and the president would relocate for ten years to Philadelphia, a move they would begin the following month.

Although they caused a lot of controversy, these were hardly the only problems to face the new government. One of the major disappointments of Washington's first term was his effort to establish peaceful relations with American Indian tribes. Though he felt certain that white settlement of the western lands was inevitable, Washington also believed that taking

ONE OF THE MAJOR DISAPPOINTMENTS OF WASHINGTON'S FIRST TERM WAS HIS EFFORT TO ESTABLISH PEACEFUL RELATIONS WITH AMERICAN INDIAN TRIBES.

American Indian land outright "would stain the character of the nation." Washington embarked on a plan to use federal money to purchase tribal lands, which would then be returned to the tribes as homelands. White settlement would not be allowed in those areas.

In 1790, Washington signed a treaty with the Creek nation, whose territories spread across four southern states. Because he hoped it would be a model for other agreements, that same year he issued an executive order forbidding white settlers from moving into lands guaranteed by treaty to any tribe.

But in the end, the order could not be enforced. When Georgia state legislators arranged to sell more than 15 million acres of Creek land, Washington found himself powerless to stop them. Meanwhile, as settlers pushed into tribal hunting grounds elsewhere, there was bloodshed. In 1791, warriors from the Miami and Wabash tribes attacked travelers along the Ohio and Wabash Rivers. In response, Washington sent General Arthur

IN 1791, GENERAL ARTHUR ST. CLAIR AND HIS MEN WERE OVERWHELMED BY WARRIORS OF THE MIAMI TRIBE, NEAR WHAT IS NOW FORT WAYNE, INDIANA. IN REPRISAL, ST. CLAIR DECISIVELY DEFEATED TRIBES NEAR TOLEDO, OHIO, TWO YEARS LATER.

St. Clair on an ill-fated mission. The troops were headed for a village of Miami Indians near what is now Fort Wayne, Indiana. When they arrived, St. Clair's men were defeated in a surprise attack by as many as 1,500 American Indians. Of 1,400 men in St. Clair's battalion, 623 were killed and 258 more were wounded. Washington would soon have to admit that his hope for peace with the tribes was doomed.

In New York, Martha Washington struggled with the role of First Lady. (She was not officially called the First Lady, however. That title would first be used by Dolley Madison, wife of the fourth president.) The first house the Washingtons lived in proved too small for the leader of the country. There wasn't enough room for large receptions or dinners. In February 1790, they moved to a four-story mansion with two large drawing rooms. As a way to stay in touch with the public, Washington used his home for weekly levees, open houses at which any respectably dressed man could talk with the president. But there was so much ceremony that not much real conversation could take place. There was also a by-invitation-only formal dinner every Thursday, and Martha held teas every Friday evening, to which both men and women were invited. She often made the tea and coffee herself. But though she did her best to fulfill her ceremonial roles, Martha complained that she felt "more like a state prisoner than anything else."

Early in his first term, Washington suffered some episodes of serious illness. In June 1789, a tumor that required surgery appeared on his left thigh. At that time, doctors didn't have a basic understanding of how germs entered the body. Surgeries were performed without sterilized tools and without anesthesia. For days after the painful operation, Washington lingered near death. The following May, a severe bout of influenza developed into pneumonia, which put him back in critical condition for days. It was plain the old soldier, in a job that required energy and concentration, could no longer count on his health.

Still, Washington was determined to make good on a promise he had made to visit every state. Unlike Franklin, Adams, and Jefferson, he had never set foot in Great Britain or France. But as a surveyor and a soldier, he had traveled more widely around

MARTHA WASHINGTON PRESIDED AT THE FORMAL TEA SHE HOSTED AT THE PRESIDENTIAL RESIDENCE EVERY FRIDAY FROM 7 TO 10 P.M.

America than any of the other founders. The war alone had taken him across nine states. As a southerner, he felt it important first to go north, so in October 1789 he embarked on a one-month tour of the New England states. Though he did not visit Rhode Island, which would not join the union until the Bill of Rights was adopted the following year, his journey took him through almost 60 towns and villages, with banquets, parades, receptions, and dances.

It wasn't until the summer of 1790 that Washington at last paid an official visit to Rhode Island. In Newport, he met with a Jewish merchant named Moses Seixas. Washington later sent Seixas and his congregation a letter that would be one of the most important statements of his presidency. It supported the idea of freedom of religion: "All possess alike liberty of conscience and immunities of citizenship," he wrote. More than that, he said, it was wrong to speak of "toleration" (tolerance), because the word implied that "it was by the indulgence of one class of people that another enjoyed the exercise of their inherent natural rights."

In December of that year, Hamilton rekindled the fight over his vision for the economy when he proposed his most radical idea yet—that Congress should charter a national bank. His Bank of the United States would assist in collecting taxes, handle payments on the national debt, issue notes that could be used as currency, and make loans to both the government and private businesses.

The bank was quickly approved by the Senate. But in the House, Madison attempted to derail the project, arguing that the Constitution did not empower the federal government to establish such a thing. When the House approved the bank all the same and

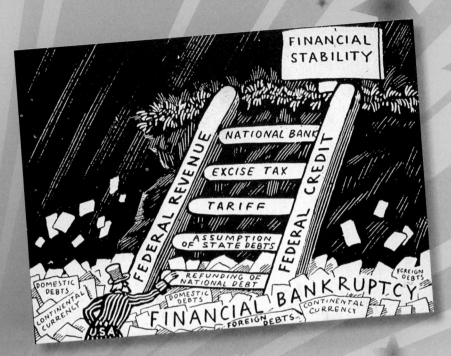

A POLITICAL CARTOON SHOWS THE STEPS THE UNITED STATES NEEDED TO TAKE TO ACHIEVE FINANCIAL STABILITY AFTER THE WAR. THE FINAL RUNG OF THE LADDER IS THE ESTABLISHMENT OF THE NATIONAL BANK.

sent the bill to the president for his signature in February 1791, Hamilton's enemies set to work to turn Washington against it. Madison urged him to veto it. Attorney General Edmund Randolph sent him a memo agreeing that it was unconstitutional. Jefferson, of course, agreed with them.

Washington decided that if he could not come up with answers to their arguments, he would veto the bill. Hamilton wrote a lengthy argument in favor of it. The bank was lawful, he declared, because the clause of the Constitution empowering the government to take all steps "necessary and proper" to execute its enumerated powers gave it "implied powers" to take measures not specifically set out in the text. Washington was convinced. He signed the bill.

THE BANK OF THE UNITED STATES WAS COMPLETED IN 1797 IN PHILADELPHIA, WHERE IT STILL STANDS.

By early 1791, Congress had completed its move to Philadelphia and was meeting in Congress Hall, next door to Independence Hall, where the Declaration of Independence had been signed. The president and his wife were living in a rented house that Washington was fitting out as a true presidential mansion. With the bank bill controversy behind him, Washington left in March for his second regional tour, this time to the southern states.

Jefferson and Madison spent part of that summer traveling together in New York State, seeking allies in their fight against Hamilton and the powerful federal government he seemed to be creating. Everywhere he looked, Jefferson saw evidence that Hamilton and his supporters were attempting to steer the young republic toward a monarchy. On the New York trip, he took the extraordinary step of recruiting Philip Freneau, a well-known poet and journalist, to move to Philadelphia, where Jefferson would see to it that he was provided with a job as a State Department translator. But his real purpose would be to start a publication, the *National Gazette*, that could become a platform for attacks on the Hamiltonian vision—and eventually on Hamilton himself. By that means, Jefferson and Madison hoped to shape voter opinion before the next year's congressional elections and help elect representatives supporting a states' rights agenda.

Over the following year, Madison would use the pages of the *Gazette* to publish anonymous attacks on Hamilton and his policies. In one, he lamented "the increasing splendor" of

THE NATIONAL GAZETTE BECAME A TIRELESS CRITIC OF HAMILTON'S, AND LATER WASHINGTON'S, POLICIES.

the executive branch. In another, he complained that the wealthiest few were accumulating more and more riches and claimed that Hamilton and his allies were partial to the rich.

It did not help that in December 1791, Hamilton delivered a new report, this one on "manufactures," which he regarded as essential to the future of the nation. In this report, he proposed all kinds of government aid to business, including direct subsidies, rewards for inventions, targeted tariffs, and improved roads and river transport. Manufacturing, he expected, would take place largely in the North, with southern states supplying raw materials. Women and children would become part of the factory workforce.

This time, however, Hamilton did not win the support of the president. Though Washington shared his enthusiasm for the growth of manufacturing in America, he considered much of Hamilton's proposal to be unconstitutional. And anyway, he said, it did not "comport with the temper of the times"—another way of saying that the country, which was still mostly agricultural, wasn't ready to be pushed headlong into the industrial future. Congress took no action on Hamilton's plan.

As 1792 opened, the first political parties in America were beginning to form. On one side were Hamilton and those of his outlook, who would come to be called Federalists. On the other were Madison, Jefferson, and their allies, who would eventually become known as Republicans (not the same as today's Republicans). All through that year, the argument between Hamilton and Madison and Jefferson intensified. Madison and Jefferson's publishing campaign continued. Hamilton wrote anonymous articles in reply.

Washington could not stop the squabble. In May, Jefferson sent Washington a letter accusing Hamilton of sapping the nation's morality by introducing a spirit of gambling and vice, and warning that he wanted to establish a monarchy.

Washington chose that moment to send out signals that he was thinking of not standing for reelection that fall. When he took the presidency, he had planned to remain in office for no more than two years, just enough time to get the country up and running. Now he poured out his heart in conversations with Jefferson and Madison, complaining that his health was failing, his eyesight dimming, his memory growing faulty. He was tired of

THE WORK FLOOR OF AMERICA'S FIRST COTTON MILL, ESTABLISHED IN 1790 IN PAWTUCKET, RHODE ISLAND. HAMILTON STRONGLY FAVORED USING FEDERAL POWER TO PROMOTE THE GROWTH OF MANUFACTURING.

the constant accusations that he wanted to establish a monarchy. He wanted to get back to Mount Vernon, especially because his favorite nephew, George Augustine Washington, was dying of tuberculosis. Explaining that he wanted to spend what was left of his life "in ease and tranquility," in May he asked Madison—whom he still did not know was the author of the anonymous attacks on Hamilton in the *National Gazette*—to draft a farewell address.

HAMILTON, MADISON, AND JEFFERSON DID NOT AGREE ON MUCH. BUT THEY ALL AGREED THAT WASHINGTON MUST BE PERSUADED TO SERVE A SECOND TERM.

Hamilton, Madison, and Jefferson did not agree on much. But they all agreed that Washington must be persuaded to serve a second term. Without him, the conflict between Federalists and Republicans could tear the country apart. By June, Madison had drafted the farewell speech that Washington had requested. But he begged the president to reconsider. Jefferson and Hamilton did likewise, even as they continued to attack each other all summer. "North and South will hang together," Jefferson told him, "if they have you to hang on."

Washington spent the summer exchanging earnest letters with his advisers. In August, he was warning Hamilton that if he could not cool his arguments with Jefferson, "I do not see . . . how the union of the states can be much longer preserved." In a letter to Jefferson, he begged for an end to "wounding suspicions and irritable charges." At a breakfast meeting with Jefferson at Mount Vernon in October, he took the opportunity to insist once again that Jefferson's fears of monarchy were overblown, that there were "not . . . ten men in the U.S. whose opinions were worth attention who entertained such a thought."

At that meeting, Washington also told Jefferson that he was willing to reconsider his decision to step down. But even then he wasn't sure. What might have pushed him at last to make a decision was a letter from his favorite female friend, Elizabeth Powel, wife of the wealthy Philadelphia businessman Samuel Powel. Intelligent, sophisticated, and shrewd about politics—she was a devoted Federalist—she enjoyed a bantering relationship with Washington. But the letter she sent him in November 1792 was fully in earnest. She warned that if he stepped down, enemies who were previously afraid to attack him publicly would feel free. They would argue that "ambition had been the moving spring of all [his] actions." She insisted that he was "the only man in America that dares to do right on all public occasions."

Washington didn't need to declare his candidacy. Simply by not announcing his retirement, he signaled his willingness to serve another term. The next month, the Electoral College returned him to office with another unanimous vote. Vice President John Adams, who was increasingly identified with the Federalists, was also reelected. With a heavy but now more experienced heart, Washington would continue for a while longer his travels on "untrodden ground."

Building a Capital

CONGRESS TRUSTED GEORGE WASHINGTON WITH MOST OF THE IMPORTANT DECISIONS ABOUT THE NATION'S CAPITAL CITY. IN JULY 1790, CONGRESS DECREED THAT THE NEW CAPITAL WOULD BE A DISTRICT OF 10 SQUARE MILES, LOCATED SOMEWHERE ON A 65-MILE-LONG STRIP OF THE POTOMAC RIVER. THE LAWMAKERS THEN LEFT IT TO WASHINGTON TO CHOOSE THE EXACT SITE.

WASHINGTON SELECTED THE SOUTHERNMOST POINT OF THE RIVERSIDE STRETCH. HE ALSO CHOSE THE PRINCIPAL PLANNER OF THE NEW CITY. PIERRE CHARLES L'ENFANT, A FRENCH MILITARY ENGINEER WHO HAD SERVED IN THE CONTINENTAL ARMY, HAD WRITTEN TO WASHINGTON IN 1789, PROPOSING HIMSELF FOR THE JOB. L'ENFANT OVERLAID A GRID PLAN (FAVORED BY THOMAS JEFFERSON) WITH THE WEB OF CIRCLES, SQUARES, AND DIAGONAL AVENUES THAT CHARACTERIZES THE CITY TODAY.

L'ENFANT DREW INSPIRATION FROM THE FRENCH PALACE OF VERSAILLES, WHERE HE HAD SPENT PART OF HIS CHILDHOOD AS THE SON OF A PAINTER SERVING KING LOUIS XV. IT WAS ALSO HIS IDEA TO BUILD THE WIDE CENTRAL LAWN THAT IS NOW THE NATIONAL MALL, WITH THE CAPITOL SITTING ON JENKINS HILL AT ITS EASTERN END AND THE PRESIDENT'S HOME ATOP A NORTH-SOUTH CROSS STREET ON THE WESTERN END.

IN 1791, A THREE-MEMBER COMMISSION, WHICH HAD BEEN FORMED TO OVERSEE THE PROJECT, DECIDED TO NAME THE NEW CAPITAL WASHINGTON. HAVING DRAWN UP THE CITY PLAN, L'ENFANT EXPECTED ALSO TO DESIGN THE CHIEF BUILDINGS. BUT HE WAS SO DIFFICULT TO WORK WITH THAT HE WAS FIRED. IN 1792, THE COMMISSION HELD A COMPETITION FOR THE DESIGN OF THE CAPITOL BUILDING. THE WINNER WAS A PHYSICIAN, DR. WILLIAM THORNTON, WHOSE DESIGN CALLED FOR A COLUMNED PORCH AND A ROTUNDA. WASHINGTON LIKED THE ROTUNDA BECAUSE IT RECALLED BUILDINGS IN ANCIENT ROME. HE AND JEFFERSON COMMENDED THORNTON'S DESIGN TO THE COMMISSIONERS, WHO TOOK THE HINT AND APPROVED THE PLAN, WHICH WASHINGTON CALLED A PERFECT BALANCE OF "GRANDEUR, SIMPLICITY, AND CONVENIENCE." IN SEPTEMBER 1793, WASHINGTON HIMSELF LAID THE CORNERSTONE FOR THE CAPITOL. TODAY, NO ONE KNOWS WHERE THAT CORNERSTONE IS.

ABOVE: L'ENFANT'S PLAN FOR WASHINGTON, D.C.
RIGHT: THE CAPITOL BUILDING TODAY.
BELOW: THORNTON'S SKETCH FOR THE FRONT OF THE BUILDING.

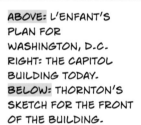

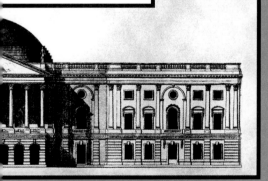

A PERFECT BALANCE OF "GRANDEUR, SIMPLICITY, AND CONVENIENCE."

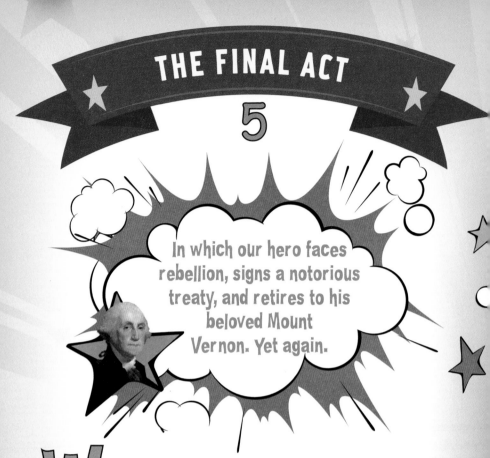

In which our hero faces rebellion, signs a notorious treaty, and retires to his beloved Mount Vernon. Yet again.

Washington's second inauguration was very different from the first. Hostility between the Federalists and Republicans had taken over. Some had complained that events such as the weekly levees at Washington's home and public celebrations of his birthday were too much like the activities of a king. Not wanting to stoke the flames, Washington kept things low key. On March 4, 1793, he traveled unaccompanied to Congress Hall, took the oath of office, and then delivered

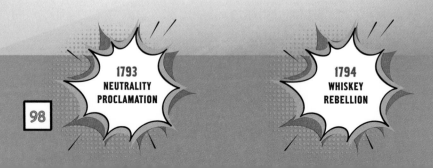

1793
NEUTRALITY
PROCLAMATION

1794
WHISKEY
REBELLION

GILBERT STUART PAINTED THIS FAMOUS PORTRAIT OF WASHINGTON IN 1796. THE IMAGE IS FULL OF SYMBOLISM, FROM HIS RELATIVELY HUMBLE DRESS INDICATING HIS NON-ROYAL STATUS TO THE SWORD REPRESENTING HIS MILITARY SERVICE.

1795
SIGNED
JAY
TREATY

1796
PUBLISHED
FAREWELL
ADDRESS

WASHINGTON ARRIVED UNACCOMPANIED AT CONGRESS HALL FOR HIS SECOND INAUGURATION.

an inaugural address that remains the shortest in history, just 135 words.

Washington's second term would be dominated by foreign affairs. Great Britain was still an adversary, but America needed it as a trading partner. France, which had been a powerful wartime ally, was now embroiled in a fast-moving revolution of its own. America would have to redefine its relations with both countries.

Just as they did with domestic disputes, Washington's cabinet members Hamilton and Jefferson went head-to-head on foreign relations. In 1784, the Continental Congress had sent Jefferson as its envoy to France. He had remained there for five happy years, long enough to witness the first days of the French Revolution in the summer of 1789. Even as it descended into bloodshed, Jefferson remained convinced that the French uprising was evidence that the American ideals of liberty and democracy were universal. Hamilton, on the other hand, viewed the French Revolution as a dangerous eruption of democratic passions. He greatly admired Britain and was anxious to repair relations as quickly as possible.

On January 31, 1793, France declared war on Great Britain. Britain responded with a blockade of France. That left the United States with a dilemma. In 1778, France and the United States had promised to defend each other against England. Hamilton urged Washington to suspend the treaty in which America had made

IN 1793, A FRENCH ARISTOCTRAT WAS BEHEADED BY GUILLOTINE DURING THE BLOODY REVOLUTION IN FRANCE. DURING WASHINGTON'S SECOND TERM, AMERICANS WERE DIVIDED ON THE QUESTION OF RELATIONS WITH FRANCE.

that promise. He argued that the treaty had been made with a monarch. That monarch had lost his throne.

Though Washington was grateful for French assistance during the war, he was also unnerved by the militants who had taken over during the French Revolution. His close friend Lafayette, though an early supporter of the uprising, had been forced to flee to Belgium. Arrested there by Austrian forces in 1792, he had been taken back to Austria and thrown into a small, filthy cell, where he would languish for five years. Washington was also receiving regular reports from Paris from his minister to France, Gouverneur Morris, who was skeptical about the path the revolution was taking.

Washington knew it would be a disaster for his young nation to become involved again so soon in war with England. On April 22, 1793, he declared American neutrality—he issued a proclamation saying that both the American government and private citizens were forbidden to take actions on behalf of either France or Britain.

GENET.

EDMUND–CHARLES GENÊT, THE FRENCH ENVOY TO AMERICA, WORKED TO UNDERMINE WASHINGTON'S POLICY OF NEUTRALITY IN THE WAR BETWEEN FRANCE AND ENGLAND.

But many Americans were pro-France. The French envoy to America, Edmond-Charles Genêt, had arrived in America on April 8. He was greeted with banquets and cheering crowds from the Carolinas to Philadelphia. In the coming months, Genêt would be a thorn in Washington's side. He equipped American ships to serve as privateers, attacking British ships in the name of France. He also developed a plan to raise an American army to take New Orleans from Spain.

By June, Genêt was becoming intolerable. Despite the ban on privateering, Genêt arranged to put cannons and an American crew on a British merchant vessel that the French had captured and towed into port at Philadelphia. Incredibly, he even claimed that the crew members were such patriots that they would use force to resist any attempt to keep them from setting sail. Soon he was promising to go over Washington's head and appeal directly to the American people. The *Gazette* cheered him on and issued warnings to the president that he had lost his position as the symbol of the American Revolution and its ideals.

Things were coming to a head. Throughout the month of July, anti-Federalist mobs roamed the streets of Philadelphia and even marched on the presidential mansion. (Decades later, John Adams would recall "the terrorism excited by Genêt.") On July 23, Washington called a cabinet meeting to discuss whether to ask France to recall its impertinent envoy. At another meeting, Secretary of War Henry Knox showed Washington a cartoon in the *Gazette* that pictured the president being carted to the guillotine. It sent him into a sputtering rage.

Later that month, the cabinet voted unanimously to demand Genêt's recall. By that time, the French, for reasons of their own, had already put a new envoy aboard a ship to America. The new French envoy, Jean Antoine Joseph Fauchet, had been directed to send Genêt home to face charges of crimes against the revolution. As much as he despised Genêt, Washington knew that to force him back to France would be a death sentence. He granted him asylum. Genêt would spend the rest of his life in upstate New York.

In that same summer of 1793, Philadelphia was gripped by a terrible epidemic of yellow fever. By October, a tenth of the

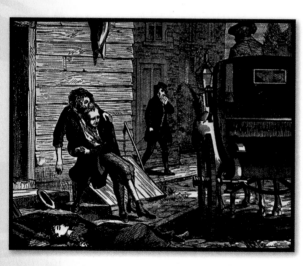

WHEN YELLOW FEVER HIT PHILADELPHIA IN 1793, THOUSANDS FLED. BANKER STEPHEN GIRARD, SEEN HERE CARRYING A VICTIM, BECAME A LOCAL HERO BY STAYING TO HELP THE SICK.

city's 35,000 people had fallen victim to the disease, and many others had fled. Having left the month before with Martha for Mount Vernon, Washington decided Congress should meet temporarily in another city.

As the dreary year drew to a close, Jefferson resigned as secretary of state on December 31. And though the onset of winter had ended the yellow fever epidemic by eliminating the mosquitoes that carried it, there was no end of new challenges.

For years, pirates from the Barbary city-states of Algiers, Tripoli, and Tunis had been preying on American ships off the coast of North Africa, seizing their crews for ransom. To combat them, in March 1794, Congress approved a measure backed by Washington to build six warships. It was effectively the beginning of the U.S. Navy.

A far greater crisis would break out later that year. To help pay for Hamilton's plan to have the federal government assume state debt, Congress had imposed a tax on whiskey in 1791. This angered grain farmers, especially in western Pennsylvania, where many kept small stills that converted their corn to liquor. By the summer of 1794, discontent had turned into the Whiskey Rebellion. When a revenue inspector named Colonel John Neville tried to serve court orders on backwoodsmen who had not registered their stills as the law required, they responded by setting fire to his house.

On August 1, 6,000 frontiersmen assembled outside Pittsburgh on Braddock's Field, near where Washington had fought in the Battle of the Monongahela during the French and Indian War. They listened to speeches denouncing the tax and daring the government to come after them. Washington took the dare. He believed the unrest was being encouraged by the Republican societies that had sprung up in the previous year in several parts of the country, especially in Pennsylvania. Activist political clubs, they were anti-Federalist and pro-French. At the August rally, some protesters even built mock guillotines in the field.

By August 7, Washington had called for New Jersey, Pennsylvania,

WASHINGTON PERSONALLY REVIEWED THE FORCES GATHERED TO PUT DOWN THE WHISKEY REBELLION.

and Virginia to mobilize 13,000 militia members. He also sent out three commissioners to attempt peace talks with the rebels. When they were rebuffed, Washington decided to lead the militia forces against the rebels himself. It is the only time in history that a sitting American president has personally supervised a military operation. In late September, Washington and Hamilton

> **IT IS THE ONLY TIME IN HISTORY THAT A SITTING AMERICAN PRESIDENT HAS PERSONALLY SUPERVISED A MILITARY OPERATION.**

left Philadelphia together by carriage. A few days later, they reached Carlisle, Pennsylvania, where the troops were gathered. The old general climbed into the saddle to review them on horseback.

There would be no real military confrontation. When they found out about the forces gathered against them, the rebels gave in. By late October, Washington was back in Philadelphia, leaving Hamilton in charge of the forces near Pittsburgh. Two rebel leaders were tried and sentenced to death, but Washington granted them clemency.

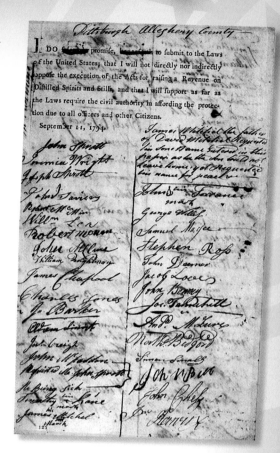

REBELS WERE FREED IF THEY SIGNED AN OATH PROMISING NOT TO IMPEDE TAX COLLECTION.

The next year of Washington's presidency would be consumed by another foreign policy controversy. The Treaty of Paris that ended the Revolutionary War did not settle all the issues in relations between the United States and Britain. Because America had failed to repay prewar debts still owed to British merchants, the British refused to honor obligations to leave forts around the Great

Lakes, where they stirred up trouble with American Indian tribes. And they permitted American goods to enter the British West Indies only on British vessels. The last straw came when the British navy began to seize American ships carrying French goods or bound for any French port. Britain did not announce this new policy until it had already been in effect for three months. Hundreds of unsuspecting American ships en route to the French West Indies were seized and sent to Britain's Caribbean islands, where their crew members were given a choice between joining the British navy or being incarcerated in disease-ridden prison ships.

Fearing that tensions were heading toward war, Washington sent Chief Justice John Jay, the president's former foreign secretary who was now chief justice on the Supreme Court, to London to negotiate a settlement. It was an unpopular decision. Many Americans could not abide the idea of negotiating anything with the hated British. Virginians were particularly wary of Jay because he supported repaying those prewar debts to British merchants, most of which were owed by Virginia planters.

In March 1795, the Jay Treaty arrived in Philadelphia. It appeared to give the British everything they wanted and the

Americans very little. Knowing it would cause controversy, Washington decided to keep the contents of the treaty secret until the Senate could debate and vote on it in June. The treaty was approved after a few weeks, but by a narrow vote of 20 to 10.

When the text was made public, it set off a fury. In Boston, a British ship was set afire in the harbor. In Philadelphia, a crowd surrounded the presidential mansion and

PROTESTERS BURNED JOHN JAY IN EFFIGY IN REACTION TO THE JAY TREATY.

demanded war with England, while another smashed windows at the home of the British minister to the United States. A mob in New York burned a copy of the treaty in front of Jay's home. He later joked that he could have traveled that summer all down the eastern seaboard by the light of the fires burning him in effigy.

Washington, who thought the treaty was the best deal America could get, acknowledged, "At present the cry against the treaty is like that against a mad dog; and everyone, in a manner, seems engaged in running it down."

On August 14, Washington announced to his cabinet that he would sign the Jay Treaty. In April 1796, the House tried to withhold funding to put the treaty into effect. It also demanded that the president turn over copies of Jay's diplomatic instructions. Sensing "a dangerous precedent" for relations between the executive and legislative branches, Washington refused. In the end, the House approved the treaty, but barely: the vote was 51 to 48. Jefferson credited the victory in Congress, which he considered a policy disaster, to Washington's esteem in the eyes of the public. In a letter to Madison, he quoted a line from Washington's favorite play, Joseph Addison's *Cato*: "A curse on his virtues, they have undone his country."

By the summer of 1796, in response to the Jay Treaty, France began to pursue and seize American ships. A newspaper published documents that purported to show that Washington had accepted bribes from the British during the Revolutionary War. The claim was based on British forgeries cooked up during the war to discredit Washington, a fact that had already been documented, but an exasperated Washington found himself forced to point this out.

It was all too much—the attacks in Congress, the constant insults in the Republican press. Exhausted and discouraged, the aging president was finished with public life. Determined not to stand for another term, Washington enlisted Hamilton to draft a farewell address, which he himself then carefully rewrote. It was never delivered as a speech but instead was published in the fall of 1796 in newspapers and as a pamphlet.

THE TIMES; A POLITICAL PORTRAIT.

Triumph Government; perish all its enemies.
Traitors be warned; justice though slow is sure.

NOT ALL POLITICAL CARTOONS CRITICIZED WASHINGTON. THIS ONE FROM 1798 SHOWS HIM RETURNING IN TRIUMPH TO LEAD HIS FORCES, WHILE THOMAS JEFFERSON TRIES IN VAIN TO HOLD BACK HIS CARRIAGE.

The address was Washington's final statement to his fellow Americans of his principles and his hopes for their future. He warned against the dangers of division. He made a case for federal power. In foreign affairs, he emphasized that states have interests, not permanent friends: "Nations as well as individuals act for their own benefit, and not for the benefit of others."

Two subjects were left out of the address: relations with American Indian tribes, which Washington had tried and failed to help, and slavery, a topic on which his own views had shifted greatly over the years. He now recognized that slavery was wrong

A FAMILY PORTRAIT FROM 1796 SHOWS GEORGE AND MARTHA WASHINGTON WITH THEIR GRANDCHILDREN, GEORGE WASHINGTON PARKE CUSTIS AND ELEANOR PARKE CUSTIS, THE YOUNGEST CHILDREN OF MARTHA'S SON, JACKY, WHO CAME TO LIVE WITH THE WASHINGTONS AFTER JACKY'S DEATH.

and insupportable, but he still feared that raising the issue too aggressively could tear apart the nation. It was a matter he would have time to think about further on his return to Mount Vernon.

The election of 1796 made John Adams president and Thomas Jefferson vice president. The executive branch would be divided between a Federalist (Adams) and a Republican (Jefferson). After his inauguration on March 4, 1797, Adams wrote of the outgoing president, "He seemed to me to enjoy a triumph over me. Methought I heard him say, 'Ay! I am fairly out and you fairly in! See which of us will be happiest!'"

⭐

Five days later, Washington and his extended family started the journey back to Mount Vernon, which was greatly in need of attention. But once again, Washington's retirement would be cut short. The French assaults on American shipping continued, which led Congress to restore the American army, disbanded after the war, and expand it by ten regiments, with the option to call up more. When President Adams sent three American commissioners to France to negotiate, they were kept waiting for three months. Then one of them wrote back to Adams with the news that the members of the Directory, the revolutionary committee that now governed France, had demanded a large bribe before they would agree to talk. The XYZ Affair—so called because three French agents identified only by those letters had been sent to extract the bribe—inflamed anti-French opinion in America. Talk of war escalated. Newspapers reported as fact rumors that the French planned a land invasion.

WITHOUT CONSULTING HIM, ADAMS NAMED WASHINGTON HEAD OF THE NEW ARMY IN JULY 1798.

Once more, Washington was drawn into events. Without consulting him, Adams named Washington head of the new army in July 1798. The old general set to work selecting his officers. This quickly created a crisis with Adams, because Washington insisted that his second-in-command should be Hamilton, whom Adams had long regarded as a rival.

Adams, who didn't believe that France was likely to invade and who had begun to see the new army as a tool of the scheming Hamilton, decided to defuse the situation. In February 1799, he announced his intention to name another commission to seek negotiations with France. War fury gradually abated. Before the tailors could complete the embroidery on Washington's new dress uniform, he withdrew.

This time he really was returning permanently to Mount Vernon. He resisted a last-ditch effort mounted by Federalists to get him to run for president again because they feared—rightly, as it turned out—that Adams was a weak and unpopular leader and that Jefferson might succeed him. Washington wanted only to get his own affairs in order. In July, working alone in his study, he started to prepare his will.

He calculated his estate to include 51,000 acres of land all around the country. He divided Mount Vernon into five plots, with different heirs for each. And then there was the question of his slaves. Washington had argued privately for years that slavery was not only wrong, it was also bad for business, since it required slave owners to provide food, shelter, and other needs for numerous enslaved people who were too old or too young to work. All the while, he had remained one of those owners unwilling, for whatever combination of reasons, to set what would have been a powerful example by freeing his slaves. There were 317 enslaved people at Mount Vernon, of which he owned 124. He was ready at last to act.

Washington decreed that at Martha's death, the slaves he owned fully should be freed. He directed that for the rest of their lives, the elderly former slaves should be "comfortably clothed and fed." The young ones should be supported until age 25, taught to read, and trained in occupations. His personal servant, Billy Lee, was to be freed immediately on Washington's death and provided with room and board. It had taken him a lifetime, but Washington had come to the right place.

It was a lifetime drawing to a close. Though December 12, 1799, was a wet, snowy day, Washington made a five-hour inspection tour of his farms on horseback. When he arrived home, there were guests waiting for him, so he remained in his damp clothes rather than delay their dinner. The next day, with snow still falling, he headed down to the banks of the Potomac to mark trees he wanted cut. That night, he awoke with throat pain and labored breathing.

A 19TH–CENTURY IMAGINING OF THE SCENE AROUND WASHINGTON'S
DEATHBED AT MOUNT VERNON IN DECEMBER 1799. HE WAS 67 YEARS OLD
WHEN HE DIED.

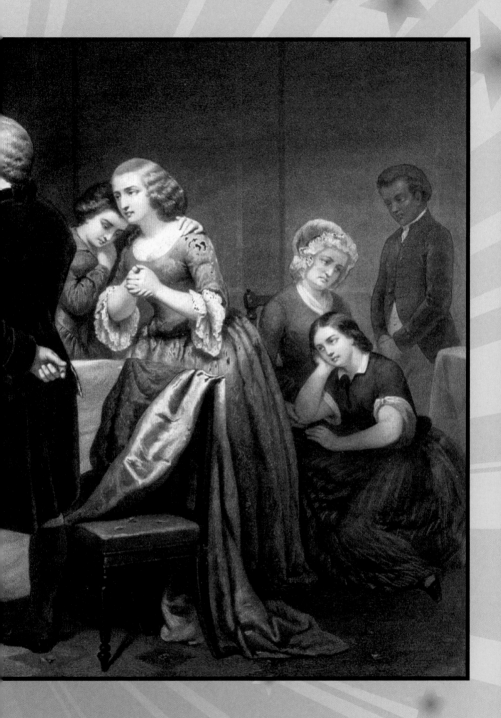

HIS SECRETARY, TOBIAS LEAR, WOULD REPORT THAT WASHINGTON DIED WHILE TAKING HIS OWN PULSE.

By the next morning, December 14, he could scarcely breathe. By the evening, he was gone. His secretary, Tobias Lear, would report that Washington died while taking his own pulse. If he did, it was the last act of a man accustomed to being in charge.

Three days later, Washington was given a military funeral at Mount Vernon. There was a band, and cannons fired, but there was no lavish ceremony. Martha, heartbroken, remained in her room.

On the day after Christmas, there was a more public memorial service in Philadelphia. A large procession moved from Congress Hall to the German Lutheran Church, where General Henry Lee, one of Washington's old wartime comrades, delivered what would turn out to be a famous description of the general. Washington, he said, was "first in war, first in peace, first in the hearts of his countrymen."

More than two centuries later, that still sounds right.

THE WASHINGTON MONUMENT IN WASHINGTON, D.C., MEMORIALIZES THE NATION'S FIRST PRESIDENT.

A note on the speech bubbles in this book

Washington and his contemporaries really did say the things that appear in speech bubbles throughout this book, although the artwork does not necessarily depict the moment at which the statements were originally made.

Page 17

"There is a Destiny which has the control of our actions, not to be resisted by the strongest efforts of Human Nature."

George Washington wrote this to his neighbor Sarah "Sally" Fairfax on September 12, 1758. Sally was the wife of George's benefactor and friend George William Fairfax. Washington had been romantically interested in Sally Fairfax even though she was already married when he met her. In the letter, Washington appears to be talking about his soon-to-be-wife, Martha Custis, but many historians believe that he was really expressing his love for Sally. If that's true, then Washington's line about destiny is likely expressing his frustration at his inability to choose his first love.

Page 21

"By the all-powerful dispensations of Providence, I have been protected . . . ; for I had four bullets through my coat, and two horses shot under me, yet escaped unhurt."

George Washington wrote this to his brother, John Washington, on July 18, 1755. The letter was a brief report on the battle at Fort Necessity.

Page 42

"There is nothing so likely to produce peace as to be well prepared to meet an enemy."

George Washington wrote this in a letter to Elbridge Gerry dated January 29, 1780. Gerry was a member of the Continental Congress and had sat on the board that oversaw finances for the Congress. Gerry had expressed to Washington that he felt the Continental Army did not need any more recruits. This was Washington's reply.

Page 48

"My brave fellows, you have done all I asked you to do, and more than can be reasonably expected; but your country is at stake, your wives, your houses and all that you hold dear."

George Washington said this to his troops on December 31, 1776. Although the Continental Army had just had a huge victory at Trenton, it had been a year of defeats. Washington's troops were only committed to serve through the end of the year. He had to persuade them to reenlist so he would have an army the next day. On the 31st, he made an impassioned plea to his officers, saying "My brave fellows, you have done all I asked you to do, and more than can be reasonably expected; but your country is at stake, your wives, your houses and all that you hold dear. You have worn yourselves out with fatigues and hardships, but we know not how to spare you. If you will consent to stay one month longer, you will render that service to the cause of liberty, and to your country, which you probably can never do under any other circumstances."

Page 57

"Having now finished the work assigned me, I retire from the great theatre of Action."

George Washington said this on December 23, 1787, in a speech to the Continental Congress at the Maryland State House in Annapolis. He was resigning his commission in the Continental Army following his army's victory in the war.

Page 64

"Heroes have made poets, and poets heroes."

George Washington wrote this in a letter to his friend the marquis de Lafayette on May 28, 1788. In the letter, Washington argued for supporting the arts. This statement made the case that artists are essential in preserving and promoting the legacies of great men.

Page 80

"Liberty may be endangered by the abuses of liberty, as well as by the abuses of power."

James Madison wrote this in an essay under the pseudonym Publius. After the Constitution was written, it needed to be ratified by at least nine states before it could take effect. James Madison, John Jay, and Alexander Hamilton wrote a series of essays to sway their fellow New Yorkers to vote in favor of the new documents. Later, these essays were gathered together into what became known as *The Federalist.* This quote was written by Madison in Federalist no. 63.

"The Nation which can prefer disgrace to danger is prepared for a Master and deserves one."

Alexander Hamilton wrote this in a letter that was published in the *Philadelphia Daily Advertiser* on February 21, 1797. The letter was intended to warn Americans against the dangers of a continuing alliance with France.

Page 81

"The whole art of government consists in the art of being honest."

Thomas Jefferson wrote this in July 1774 in an essay entitled, "A Summary View of the Rights of British America."

Page 86

"I live a very dull life here . . . Indeed I think I am more like a state prisoner than anything else."

Martha Washington wrote this in a letter to her niece Fanny on October 23, 1789, less than six months after George's inauguration. In the letter, Martha described a watch and some fabric that she was sending to Fanny, and told her that she couldn't tell Fanny what was fashionable in New York, because she never went into town. "Mrs Sims will give you a better account of the fashons than I can," she wrote. "I live a very dull life hear and know nothing that passes in the town–I never goe to the publick place–indeed I think I am more like a state prisoner than anything else, there is certain bounds set for me which I must not depart from–and as I can not doe as I like I am obstinate and stay at home a great deal."

Page 99

"Gentlemen, you will permit me to put on my spectacles, for, I have grown not only gray, but almost blind in the service of my country."

George Washington said this during his address at Newburgh, New York, on March 15, 1783. Military officers, disgruntled by

Congress's refusal to give them back pay, had gathered there. Washington gave an impassioned speech for patience. Many of the officers were moved to tears by their former commander's admission that he was growing frail.

Page 116
"'Tis well."

After his death, George Washington's secretary, Tobias Lear, wrote a journal entry that described the events surrounding it. According to Lear, Washington remained calm and concerned as he approached death, refusing to let Martha go for help at night because he worried that she might catch a cold. According to Lear, Washington's last words were, "'Tis well."

Excerpts from the Writings of George Washington

George Washington was a prolific writer. Throughout his life, he recorded his life and thoughts in diaries and letters that form one of the most extensive archives of any figure from the 18th century. Washington's words were also recorded by other figures from the time. These excerpts, which are reprinted with Washington's abbreviations and misspellings intact, reveal a man who was both dedicated to his principles and acutely aware of the legacy his writings would build.

On His Undying Affection

September 12, 1758, to Sarah "Sally" Fairfax

SARAH "SALLY" FAIRFAX

When Washington's half brother Lawrence married into the wealthy Fairfax family, a world of possibilities was opened to George. When he was sixteen, Sarah "Sally" Fairfax married Washington's friend and benefactor George William Fairfax. She is credited with refining Washington's manners, teaching him, among other things, how to dance the minuet. Historians believe that Washington loved Sally Fairfax, and many interpret this letter, in which Washington seems to be describing his love for Martha before their marriage, as a veiled declaration of love for Sally.

Tis true, I profess myself a Votary to Love—I acknowledge that a Lady is in the Case—and further I confess, that this Lady is known to you.—Yes Madam, as well as she is to one, who is too sensible of her Charms to deny the Power, whose Influence he feels and must ever Submit to. I feel the force of her amiable beauties in the recollection of a thousand tender passages that I coud wish to obliterate, till I am bid to revive them.—but experience alas! sadly reminds me how Impossible this is.—and evinces an Opinion which I have long entertain'd, that there is a Destiny, which has the Sovereign controul of our Actions—not to be resisted by the strongest efforts of Human Nature.

You have drawn me my dear Madam, or rather have I drawn myself, into an honest confession of a Simple Fact— misconstrue not my meaning—'tis obvious—doubt it not, nor expose it,—the World has no business to know the object of my Love, declard in this manner to—you when I want to conceal it—One thing, above all things in this World I wish to know, and only one person of your Acquaintance can solve me that, or guess my meaning.—but adieu to this, till happier times, if I ever shall see them.—the hours at present are melancholy dull.

On His Appointment as Commander of the Continental Army

MARTHA
WASHINGTON

June 18, 1775, to Martha Washington

When the Continental Congress named Washington as the commander in chief of the Continental Army, his first task might well have been the hardest. Washington had to tell Martha that he would not be returning to their quiet life at Mount Vernon. He wrote her an angst-filled letter, in which he confessed his anxiety over the new job, and begged her to find a way to keep herself happy in his absence.

My Dearest
I am now set down to write you on a subject which fills me with inexpressible concern—and this concern is greatly aggravated

and Increased, when I reflect upon the uneasiness I know it will give you—It has been determined in Congress that the whole Army raised for the defence of the American Cause shall be put under my care, and that it is necessary for me to proceed immediately to Boston to take upon me the command of it. You may believe me my dear Patcy, when I assure you, in the most solemn manner, that, so far from seeking this appointment I have used every endeavor in my power to avoid it, not only from my unwillingness to part with you and the Family, but from a consciousness of its being a trust too great for my Capacity and that I should enjoy more real happiness and felicity in one month with you, at home, than I have the most distant prospect of reaping abroad, if my stay were to be Seven times Seven years. But, as it has been a kind of destiny that has thrown me upon this Service, I shall hope that my undertaking of it, is designed to answer some good purpose—You might, and I suppose did perceive, from the Tenor of my letters, that I was apprehensive I could not avoid this appointment, as I did not even pretend [t]o intimate when I should return—that was the case—it was utterly out of my power to refuse this appointment without exposing my Character to such censures as would have reflected dishonour upon myself, and given pain to my friends—this, I am sure could not, and ought not be pleasing to you, & must have lessened me considerably in my own esteem. I shall rely therefore, confidently, on that Providence which has heretofore preservd, & been bountiful to me, not doubting but that I shall return safe to you in the fall—I shall feel no pain *from the Toil, or the danger of the Campaign—My unhapiness will flow, from the uneasiness I know you will feel at being left alone—I beg of you to summon your whole fortitude Resolution, and pass your time as agreeably as possible—nothing will give me so much sincere satisfaction as to hear this, and to hear it from your own pen.*

On the American Relationship with Canada

September 14, 1775, to the inhabitants of Canada

Early in the revolution, Washington sent two forces into Canada. The first would conquer Montreal, then travel north to meet up with forces led by Benedict Arnold in an attempt to seize Quebec City. The expeditions hoped to topple British leadership in Canada, but also to sway French Canadians to join the American cause. Washington wrote this address in an attempt to convince the colonies' neighbors to the north.

Friends and Brethren,
The unnatural Contest between the English Colonies and Great-Britain, has now risen to such a Heighth, that Arms alone must decide it. The Colonies, confiding in the Justice of their Cause, and the Purity of their Intentions, have reluctantly appealed to that Being, in whose Hands are all human Events. He has hitherto smiled upon their virtuous Efforts— The Hand of Tyranny has been arrested in its Ravages, and the British Arms which have shone with so much Splendor in every Part of the Globe, are now tarnished with Disgrace

and Disappointment.—Generals of approved Experience, who boasted of subduing this great Continent, find themselves circumscribed within the Limits of a single City and its Suburbs, suffering all the Shame and Distress of a Siege. While the trueborn Sons of America, animated by the genuine Principles of Liberty and Love of their Country, with increasing Union, Firmness and Discipline repel every Attack, and despise every Danger.

Above all, we rejoice, that our Enemies have been deceived with Regard to you—They have perswaded themselves, they have even dared to say, that the Canadians were not capable of distinguishing between the Blessings of Liberty, and the Wretchedness of Slavery; that gratifying the Vanity of a little Circle of Nobility—would blind the Eyes of the People of Canada.—By such Artifices they hoped to bend you to their Views, but they have been deceived, instead of finding in you that Poverty of Soul, and Baseness of Spirit, they see with a Chagrin equal to our Joy, that you are enlightned, generous, and virtuous—that you will not renounce your own Rights, or serve as Instruments to deprive your Fellow Subjects of theirs.— Come then, my Brethren, unite with us in an indissoluble Union, let us run together to the same Goal.—We have taken up Arms in Defence of our Liberty, our Property, our Wives, and our Children, we are determined to preserve them, or die. We look forward with Pleasure to that Day not far remote (we hope) when the Inhabitants of America shall have one Sentiment, and the full Enjoyment of the Blessings of a free Government.

On the Possibility of Becoming President

August 28, 1788, to Alexander Hamilton

ALEXANDER HAMILTON

In the period between the end of the Constitutional Convention and the document's ratification, Alexander Hamilton and James Madison regularly pressed Washington to consider participating in the first presidential election. To one letter from Hamilton, Washington replied that he refused to commit to the idea while the ratification of the Constitution was still in question, and insisted that he would prefer to live in retirement at Mount Vernon.

On the delicate subject with which you conclude your letter, I can say nothing; because the event alluded to may never happen; and because, in case it should occur, it would be a point of prudence to defer forming one's ultimate and irrevocable decision, so long as new data might be afforded for one to act with the greater wisdom & propriety. I would not wish to conceal my prevailing sentiment from you. For you know me well enough, my good Sir, to be persuaded that I am not guilty of affection, when I tell you, it is my great and sole desire to live and die, in peace and retirement, on my own farm. Were it even indispensable, a different line of conduct should be adopted; while you and some others who are acquainted with my heart would acquit, the world and Posterity might probably accuse me of inconsistency and ambition. Still I hope I shall always possess firmness and virtue enough to maintain (what I consider the most enviable of all titles) the character of an honest man, as well as prove (what I desire to be considered in reality) that I am, with great sincerity & esteem, Dear Sir Your friend and Most obedient Hble Ser[vant]

On His Inauguration

April 30, 1789, first inaugural address

When finally elected, unanimously, to the presidency, Washington gave a remarkably humble inaugural address.

Fellow Citizens of the Senate and the House of Representatives.

Among the vicissitudes incident to life, no event could have filled me with greater anxieties than that of which the notification was transmitted by your order, and received on the fourteenth day of the present month. On the one hand, I was summoned by my Country, whose voice I can never hear but with veneration and love, from a retreat which I had chosen with the fondest predilection, and, in my flattering hopes, with an immutable decision, as the asylum of my declining years: a retreat which was rendered every day more necessary as well as more dear to me, by the addition of habit to inclination, and of frequent interruptions in my health to the gradual waste committed on it by time. On the other hand, the magnitude and difficulty of the trust to which the voice of my Country called me, being sufficient to awaken in the wisest and most experienced of her citizens, a distrustful scrutiny into his qualifications, could not but overwhelm with dispondence, one, who, inheriting inferior endowments from nature and unpractised in the duties of civil administration, ought to be peculiarly conscious of his own deficiencies. In this conflict of emotions, all I dare aver, is, that it has been my faithful study to collect my duty from a just appreciation of every circumstance, by which it might be affected. All I dare hope, is, that, if in executing this task I have been too much swayed by a grateful remembrance of former instances, or by an affectionate sensibility to this transcendent proof, of the confidence of my fellow-citizens; and have thence too little consulted my incapacity as well as disinclination for the weighty and untried cares before me; my error will be palliated by the motives which misled me, and its consequences be judged by my Country, with some share of the partiality in which they originated.

On Religious Freedom

August 18, 1790, to the Hebrew congregation in Newport, Rhode Island

In August 1790, Washington traveled to Rhode Island. The state had been deliberately left out of his earlier tour of New England because it had not yet ratified the Constitution. Following Rhode Island's ratification, on May 29, 1790, Washington planned a trip there. In Newport, he was addressed by the town, its Christian clergy, and, unusually, the warden of the local synagogue, Moses Seixas. Seixas's address expressed his hope that religious tolerance would prevail in the new government. Washington's reply, written at a time before the first amendment, guaranteeing religious freedom, had been passed, laid important groundwork for the nation that would come.

The reflection on the days of difficulty and danger which are past is rendered the more sweet, from a consciousness that they are succeeded by days of uncommon prosperity and security. If we have wisdom to make the best use of the advantages with which we are now favored, we cannot fail, under the just administration of a good Government, to become a great and a happy people.

The Citizens of the United States of America have a right to applaud themselves for having given to mankind examples of an enlarged and liberal policy: a policy worthy of imitation. All possess alike liberty of conscience and immunities of citizenship. It is now no more that toleration is spoken of, as if it was by the indulgence of one class of people, that another enjoyed the exercise of their inherent natural rights. For happily the Government of the United States, which gives to bigotry no sanction, to persecution no assistance requires only that they who live under its protection should demean themselves as good citizens, in giving it on all occasions their effectual support.

It would be inconsistent with the frankness of my character not to avow that I am pleased with your favorable opinion of my Administration, and fervent wishes for my felicity. May the Children of the Stock of Abraham, who dwell in this land, continue to merit and enjoy the good will of the other Inhabitants; while every one shall sit in safety under his own vine and figtree, and there shall be none to make him afraid. May the father of all mercies scatter light and not darkness in our paths, and make us all in our several vocations useful here, and in his own due time and way everlastingly happy.

G. Washington

The Life and Times of George Washington

1732
BORN NEAR POPES CREEK, VIRGINIA, ON FEBRUARY 22

1748
UNDERTOOK FIRST SURVEY EXPEDITION INTO WILDERNESS TERRITORIES

1732 **1748** **1752** **1754** **1754-1758** **175**

1754
PUBLISHED *THE JOURNAL OF MAJOR GEORGE WASHINGTON*; SURRENDERED TO THE FRENCH AT FORT NECESSITY ON JULY 3

1752
LAWRENCE WASHINGTON DIED

1755
BRADDOCK DEFEA AT THE BATTLE O THE MONONGAHEL ON JULY 9

1754-1758
SERVED IN THE FREN AND INDIAN WAR

1776

CROSSED THE DELAWARE RIVER

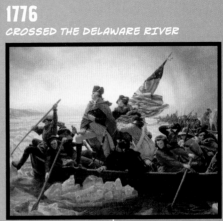

1774

SERVED AS
A DELEGATE
TO THE FIRST
CONTINENTAL
CONGRESS

59

RRIED MARTHA
NDRIDGE CUSTIS

1775

UNANIMOUSLY
CHOSEN AS
COMMANDER
OF THE
CONTINENTAL
ARMY

759 1761 1774 1775 1776 1777–1778 >

761

NHERITED MOUNT VERNON

1777–1778

SURVIVED A BITTER WINTER
AT VALLEY FORGE

1781
CORNWALLIS SURRENDERED AT YORKTOWN

1791
SIGNED BILL CHARTERING THE BANK OF THE UNITED STATES

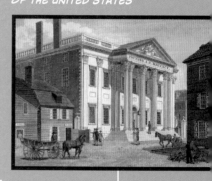

1783
RETIRED AGAIN TO MOUNT VERNON

1787
UNANIMOUSLY ELECTED PRESIDENT OF THE CONSTITUTIONAL CONVENTION

1781   1783   1786   1787   1789   179

1786
SHAYS'S REBELLION BEGAN

1789
UNANIMOUSLY ELECTED PRESIDENT OF THE UNITED STATES

92
ANIMOUSLY ELECTED TO A SECOND TERM
PRESIDENT

1796
PUBLISHED FAREWELL ADDRESS

1798
TEMPORARILY
LEFT RETIREMENT
TO ONCE AGAIN
BECOME AN ARMY
COMMANDER

1795
SIGNED JAY TREATY

792 1793 1794 1795 1796 1798 1799

1793
ISSUED NEUTRALITY
PROCLAMATION

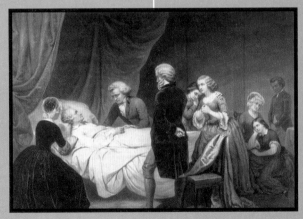

94
ED MILITIA AGAINST THE
HISKEY REBELLION

1799
DIED AT MOUNT VERNON ON DECEMBER 14

INDEX

Note: Page numbers in **bold** refer to illustrations.

ACKNOWLEDGMENTS

The text in this book was edited and condensed from *George Washington: How the Great Uniter Helped Create the United States* by Richard Lacayo, New York: Time Home Entertainment, 2011.

PICTURE CREDITS

Cover: Tim O'Brien

Pages 1: Steve Wisbauer/Getty Images; **3:** Mount Vernon Ladies' Association; **4:** Francis G. Mayer/Corbis/VCG/Getty Images; **6:** Gilbert Stuart/Getty Images; **7:** Culver Pictures; **8:** Mount Vernon Ladies' Association; **9:** Everett Collection; **10:** Everett Collection; **11:** Mount Vernon Ladies' Association; **14:** Mount Vernon Ladies' Association; **17:** Washington-Custis-Lee Collection/Washington and Lee University, Lexington, Virginia; **18:** Kean Collection/Getty Images; **20–21:** Mount Vernon Ladies' Association; **23:** Universal History Archive/UIG/Getty images; **24:** (top) VCG Wilson/Corbis/Getty Images, (bottom) Mount Vernon Ladies' Association (2); **25:** Mount Vernon Ladies' Association (2); **26:** (top) Joe Raedle/Getty Images, (middle, bottom) Mount Vernon Ladies' Association; **27:** Mount Vernon Ladies' Association (2); **28:** Gilbert Stuart/Getty Images; **29:** Mount Vernon Ladies' Association; **31:** MPI/Getty Images; **32:** Universal History Archive/Getty Images; **34:** Universal History Archive/Getty Images; **37:** Art Resource, NY; **38:** Buyenlarge/Getty Images; **39:** Interim Archives/Getty Images; **41:** Jerry Tavin/Everett Collection; **42–43:** Art Resource, NY; **45:** Eric Lessing/Art Resource, NY; **48–49:** Christie's Images/Bridgeman Images; **51, 54:** RMN-Grand Palais/Art Resource, NY; **56–57:** Yale University Art Gallery; **58:** (top) The Granger Collection, (bottom) Library of Congress; **59:** DeAgostini/Getty Images; **60:** Mount Vernon Ladies' Association; **61:** The Granger Collection; **62:** Gilbert Stuart/Getty Images; **63:** Mount Vernon Ladies' Association; **64–65:** The Metropolitan Museum of Art; **67:** The Granger Collection (2), **69:** Getty Images; **70–71:** Architect of the Capitol; **74:** Bettmann/Getty Images; **75:** (top) The Granger Collection, (bottom) North Wind Picture Archives/The Image Works; **76:** Gilbert Stuart/Getty Images; **77:** Hulton Archive/Getty Images; **78:** Mount Vernon Ladies' Association; **79:** Bettmann/Getty Images; **80:** (left) Universal History Archive/Getty Images, (right) New York Historical Society/Bridgeman Images; **81:** Bettmann/Getty Images; **84:** U.S. Army Military History Institute; **86–87:** Mount Vernon Ladies' Association; **89:** MPI/Getty Images; **90:** Corbis/Getty Images; **91:** Library of Congress; **93:** Bettmann/Getty Images; **96–97:** (top, bottom) Library of Congress, (middle) Getty Images; **98:** Gilbert Stuart/Getty Images; **99:** VCG Wilson/Corbis/Getty Images; **100:** Universal History Archive/UIG/Getty images; **101:** Corbis/Getty Images; **102:** The Granger Collection; **104:** Bettmann/Getty Images; **106, 107:** The Granger Collection; **108:** Stock Montage/Getty Images; **109:** Universal History Archive/UIG/Getty Images; **111:** Fotosearch/Getty Images; **112–13:** National Gallery of Art; **116–17:** Mount Vernon Ladies' Association; **119:** Matt McClain/The Washington Post/Getty Images; **126:** Virginia Historical Society/Bridgeman Images; **127:** Jerry Tavin/Everett Collection; **131:** New York Historical Society/Bridgeman Images; **135:** Universal History Archive/UIG/Getty Images.

Timeline: (1732) Free Library of Philadelphia/Bridgeman Images, (1748) Everett Collection, (1752, 1754) Mount Vernon Ladies' Association; (1755) Universal History Archive/Getty Images, (1759) Mount Vernon Ladies' Association, (1761) The Granger Collection, (1776) Art Resource, NY, (1777) Universal History Archive/UIG/Getty images, (1781) Ann Ronan Pictures/Print Collector/Getty Images, (1786) Bettmann/Getty Images, (1789) akg-images/The Image Works, (1791) Corbis/Getty Images, (1792) Universal History Archive/UIG/Getty Images, (1794) The Granger Collection, (1796) Library of Congress, (1799) Mount Vernon Ladies' Association.